A Guide to MS/PC DOS

Timothy N. Trainor

Jeffrey A. Stipes

M P *Mitchell Publishing, Inc.*
Innovators in Computer Education
55 Penny Lane • Watsonville, California 95076
(800) 435-2665 • In California (408) 724-0195
A Random House Company

Composition: Ideas to Images
Copy Editor: Karon French
Cover Design: Juan Vargas
Illustrations (EPS format): Mark Powell and Gary Palmatier
Interior Design: Gary Palmatier, Ideas to Images
Printer: Delta Lithograph Company
Product Development: Raleigh S. Wilson
Production Management: Ideas to Images
Sponsoring Editor: Roger L. Howell

© 1989 Mitchell Publishing, Inc.
Innovators in Computer Education

All rights reserved under International and Pan-American Copyright Conventions. No part of this book may be reproduced in any form or by any means, electronic or mechanical, including photocopying, without permission in writing from the publisher. All inquiries should be addressed to Mitchell Publishing, Inc., 55 Penny Lane, Watsonville, CA 95076, (408) 724-0195 or (800) 435-2665. Published in the United States by Mitchell Publishing, Inc., a subsidiary of Random House, Inc., New York, and simultaneously in Canada by Random House of Canada Limited, Toronto. Distributed by Random House, Inc.

Printed in the United States of America
   10 9 8 7 6 5 4 3 2 1

Library of Congress Card Catalog No: 88-063483
ISBN: 0-394-39581-6

A Guide to
MS/PC DOS

Contents

Directory of DOS Messages   IX

Preface   XI

Chapter 1: What Is DOS?   1

    Booting Your Microcomputer   2
    Microcomputer Start-Up Procedures   4
    Checking DOS Version Number   7
    DOS Commands and Utility Programs   8
    Formatting a New (or Old) Diskette   8
    Checking a Disk's Volume Label   12
    Disk Directories   14
    Clearing the Screen   19
    Backing Up Files with the Copy Command   19
    Automatically Verifying Every Copy   24
    Problem Solving with DOS   26
    Answers to Exploring DOS Questions   31

Chapter 2: The DOS Keyboard   33

    Commonly Used Keys   36
    Keys that Don't Do Anything by Themselves   37
    Activating Built-In Features   38
    Special Key Combinations   39
    Command Entry Shortcuts   40
    Problem Solving with DOS   42
    Answers to Exploring DOS Questions   45

Chapter 3: Updating 47

    Changing the System's Date   47

    Changing the System's Time   48

    Wild Card Characters   49

    Erasing or Deleting Files from Disk   51

    Renaming Disk Files   54

    Changing a Disk's Volume Label   56

    Problem Solving with DOS   59

    Answers to Exploring DOS Questions   62

Chapter 4: Text Output 63

    Displaying the Contents of a File   63

    Limiting Displays Using the More Filter   65

    Additional Copy Applications   68

    Displaying the Contents of a File on the Printer   72

    Changing Modes with which I/O Ports Operate   77

    Problem Solving with DOS   81

    Answers to Exploring DOS Questions   84

Chapter 5: Hard Disk Management 85

    Making Subdirectories   88

    Referencing Files in a Subdirectory   91

    Changing From One Subdirectory to Another   92

    Removing Subdirectories From Disk   95

    Customizing the DOS Prompt   97

    Identifying Search Paths For Programs   100

    Appending Search Paths For Data Files   103

    Backing Up Large Disk Files   106

    Restoring Files Saved with Backup Utility   113

    Problem Solving with DOS   117

    Answers to Exploring DOS Questions   122

Chapter 6: Backup and Recovery 123

    Identifying Bad Disks with CHKDSK 123
        Bad Sectors 124
        Fragmented Files 124
        Lost Clusters 125
    Diskcopy 130
    Comparing Disks 133
    Replacing Old Backups with New 136
    Setting File Attributes 140
    Recovering Lost files 143
    More on the Copy Command 146
        Uniting Fragmented Files 146
        Locating Bad Files Using Copy 147
        Recovering Bad Files Using Copy 147
    Problem Solving with DOS 149
    Answers to Exploring DOS Questions 154

Chapter 7: Customizing Your System 155

    Defining Hardware/Software Relationships 155
    Configuration Commands 156
    Creating a CONFIG.SYS File 164
    CONFIG.SYS File Errors 165
    Customizing System Operations with AUTOEXEC.BAT 166
    Problem Solving with DOS 170
    Exploring DOS Answers 176

Chapter 8: What's New with DOS 4.0 177

    Special DOS 4.0 Features 178
    Extended and Expanded Memory 179
    Word-Oriented Shell 179
    New Commands and Utilities 181
    Changes to Familiar Commands and Utilities 186
    Changes to Configuration Commands 189
    What's Next? 190

Appendices

Appendix A: Disk Drives and Media **191**
  5-1/4 Inch Floppy Disks 191
  3-1/2 Inch Diskettes 192
  Organization and Layout of Disk Media 193
  The Care and Protection of Your Disks 195

Appendix B: DOS Commands and Utilities **197**
  Configuration Commands 199
  Configuration Files 200
  Batch Commands 200

Appendix C: DOS Rules for Naming Files **201**
  Acceptable Characters for Filenames 202
  Invalid Filenames 202
  Filenaming Systems 202

Appendix D: Parallel and Serial Ports **203**
  Parallel Ports 203
  Serial Ports 204
  Differences in Data Transmission 204

Appendix E: Practical Batch Files **205**

Appendix F: Local Area Networks **209**
  What is a LAN? 209
  How Does a LAN Work? 210
  DOS Instructions that Don't Work on LANs 210

Glossary 211

Index 219

Directory of DOS Messages

APPEND 105	**MD** 90
ATTRIB 142	**MKDIR** 90
BACKUP 111	**MODE** 80
Booting Your Microcomputer 6	**MORE** 67
CD 94	**PATH** 102
CHDIR 94	**PRINT** 76
CHKDSK 128	**PROMPT** 99
CLS 19	**RD** 96
CONFIG.SYS 166	**RECOVER** 146
COPY 22, 71	**RENAME** 55
DATE 48	**REPLACE** 139
DEL 53	**RESTORE** 116
DIR 17	**RMDIR** 96
DISKCOMP 135	**SELECT** 178
DISKCOPY 132	**TIME** 49
FORMAT 11	**TYPE** 65
ERASE 53	**VER** 8
Error Codes 184	**VERIFY** 25
LABEL 57	**VOL** 13

*This book is dedicated
to the ones we love:*

Diane Krasnewich
and
Karen Stipes

Preface

Through our teaching experience, we have found that people run into hardware and software difficulties because they do not understand how to use their computer's disk operating system, or *DOS*. They may have been led to believe that mastering the commands and utilities that control their IBM and IBM-compatible microcomputers will be their worst nightmare come true; fortunately, this perception is largely unfounded. Nevertheless, difficulties *can* arise when users engage in two common actvities:

- Deciding how to use DOS to best accomplish certain tasks, such as displaying disk directories, copying files, or formatting a new disk. These tasks require the user to select and properly apply the appropriate DOS feature.

- Recovering from problems that occur when the DOS instruction used produces undesired results. Picking the right solution centers around understanding what went wrong.

This DOS Guide addresses these two challenges. It shows how to effectively apply DOS instructions and also illustrates how to correct errors by examining typical mistakes.

A GUIDE TO MS/PC DOS

This Guide introduces DOS concepts and instructions in a sequence that supports a comfortable introduction to microcomputer operations. Examples focus on DOS from version 2.0 through 4.01. Our goal is to help you become a proficient DOS user. To this end we have written a book than can be used two ways:

Easy-to-Read Introduction to DOS

The first-time computer user is taken step-by-step, progressing from the most basic DOS instructions to more sophisticated applications. Strong pedagogy typically found in text books, such as study questions (Exploring DOS) and problem sets (Problem Solving with DOS), are included in this Guide. These exercises reinforce mastery of DOS by identifying useful patterns for problem solving using DOS.

Easy-to-Use Desktop Reference

People who use DOS at home, school, or work need a sourcebook for detailed examples of screen displays, instruction formats, and explanations of DOS messages. This DOS Guide has a comprehensive glossary, index, and, in addition to the full table of contents, a page reference table for all the DOS instructions and related messages.

ORGANIZATION OF THE GUIDE

Each DOS command and utility program is explained through the use of four design features: narrative, sample screens, related DOS messages, and review questions. Simple questions like, "Do I type a space after DIR?" are answered by special illustrations that clearly identify the proper instruction syntax.

Narrative

The narrative explains the purpose of each DOS instruction and provides a description of situations where it is used. These explanations include a brief overview of what the operating system does when it executes a specific instruction and an outline of uses for optional features. Narratives are concise and to the point; as a result, you are not overwhelmed by seldomly-used features that most DOS users do not need to know.

Sample Screen Displays

Sample screen displays support the narrative by illustrating how DOS works. This type of visual aid is especially helpful when all you need is a quick glance to remind you of the correct syntax or an optional switch. One special design feature of this book is the use of color in screen displays to illustrate what you need to enter, while the black represents text generated by the computer.

DOS Messages

Special attention is paid to the screen messages DOS sends to the user. We realize that many DOS messages, especially error messages, are cryptic without a complete understanding of the computer's language. Therefore, after the introduction of each DOS instruction, a selection of common **DOS Messages** is presented, with an explanation of each message and a possible course of action when appropriate. A special directory of DOS Messages at the front of the book contains the page location of each DOS Message box for users who need quick answers to DOS problems.

Exploring DOS

You are also asked to apply what you have learned in the sections called **Exploring DOS.** These sections walk you through many of the DOS activities discussed in the Guide, from booting your system to copying files and changing the system date. The correct response to each question is found at the end of the chapter.

Problem Solving with DOS

As a proficient DOS user, you will use your knowledge of DOS to solve problems. The section entitled **Problem Solving with DOS,** found at the conclusion of each chapter, introduces you to problems commonly encountered by DOS users. A familiarity with these problems and their solutions can help you avoid them in your own computer use.

INCREASING PERSONAL PRODUCTIVITY

Whether you work directly with DOS, or through a word-oriented DOS shell (or Presentation Manager), you still need to know the basic structure of actions you wish to have carried out by the computer. This Guide will significantly enhance your use of DOS regardless of how you approach personal computing.

ACKNOWLEDGMENTS

Books like this are not developed overnight, and we would like to acknowledge those who helped us. Francis Rice of Oklahoma State and Jim Wilson of Triton College provided insightful reviews of early drafts of this DOS Guide. Jesse Sprayberry, Bruce Haase, Sandy Schwab, Ron Sieplinga, Lee Carlson, Diane Krasnewich, and Karen Stipes all provided support closer to home. Furthermore, we have received invaluable assistance and professional expertise from our editing, production, and support staff. Thank you.

                              Tim Trainor
                              Jeff Stipes
                              Muskegon, Michigan

1 What Is DOS?

IN THIS CHAPTER:

CLS
COPY
DIR
FORMAT
VER
VERIFY
VOL

Computers perform such sophisticated functions that people sometimes forget that computers are machines. All the remarkable activities computers accomplish are the result of following a set of detailed instructions that make up a computer program.

Computer programs (software) fall into two general categories: application programs and system software. ***Application programs*** provide users with information or perform a specific operation that users need completed. Game, drawing, or payroll programs are examples of applications programs. ***System software*** oversees internal computer operations and associated peripheral activities. These peripheral activities include the control of input, output, and auxiliary storage equipment. Software that copies a program from disk into the computer's memory is an example of system software.

The collection of system software that controls all the hardware within a specific computer system is known as an ***operating system.*** This reference guide will focus on the disk operating system (***DOS***) designed to operate IBM and IBM-compatible microcomputers. Developed by Microsoft Corporation, ***MS-DOS*** is the most commonly used microcomputer operating system in the world. Licensed and distributed by IBM Corporation as ***PC-DOS***, this operating system has evolved from version 1.0 through many revisions up to the current version 4.01.

BOOTING YOUR MICROCOMPUTER

The term **booting** refers to the procedures for loading the operating system from the disk into the computer's active memory. Booting occurs when a computer is switched on. IBM and compatible microcomputers automatically look for and load a command program from the operating system into memory as a part of the booting process.

Figure 1.1
One diskette system. The unit on the left has a full-height diskette drive, the one on the right a half-high drive.

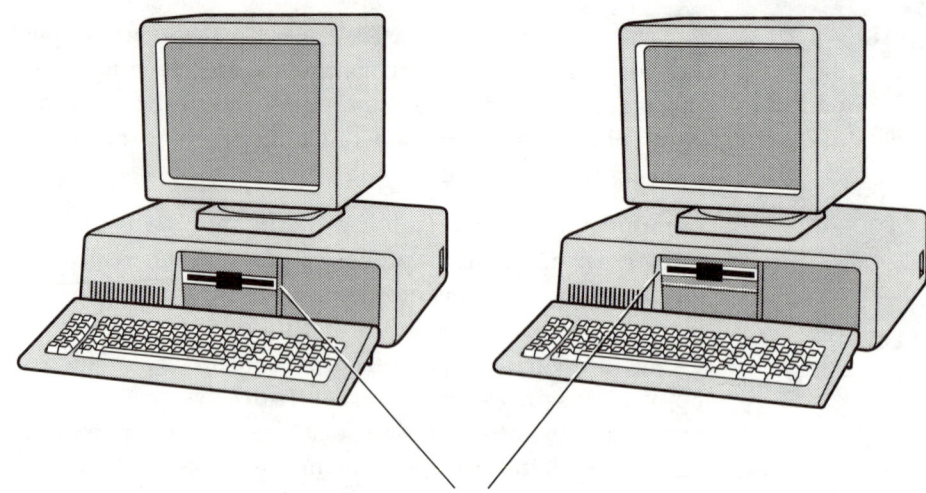

Drive A: *Both system and data drive.*

Figure 1.2
Two diskette system. This configuration allows users to run the operating system and an application from one disk and write data to the other.

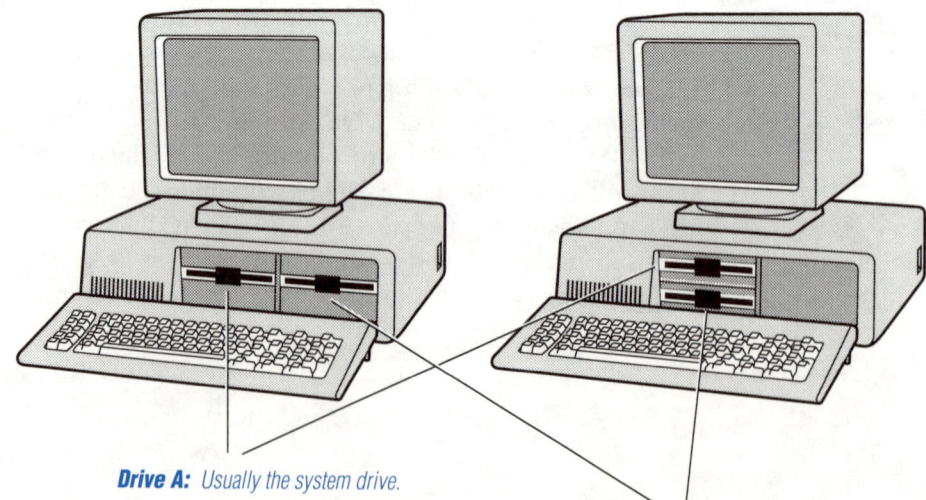

Drive A: *Usually the system drive.*

Drive B: *Usually the data drive.*

CHAPTER 1: WHAT IS DOS?   3

Since a disk with DOS must be in a designated disk drive when booting a microcomputer, associated procedures will vary depending on the number and types of disk drives. In this guide, the disk drive reading the DOS disk is referred to as the ***system drive***. Disk drives containing data (or programs) are referred to as the ***data drive***. The drive configurations illustrated in Figures 1.1 through 1.4 will help you identify the system drive used by your microcomputer system.

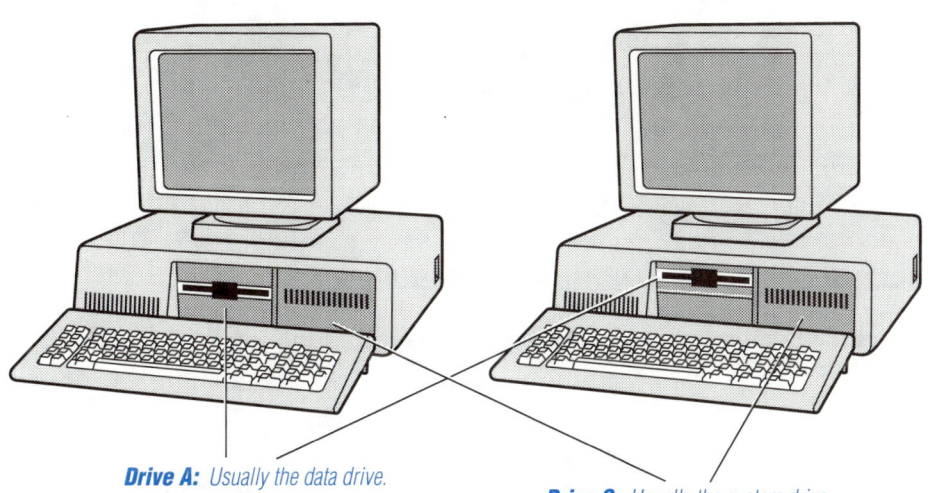

Figure 1.3
One diskette and hard disk system. DOS and your applications, as well as most of your data files, generally reside on the hard disk. The diskette drive allows users to move data in and out of the system via floppy disk.

Drive A: Usually the data drive.
Drive C: Usually the system drive.

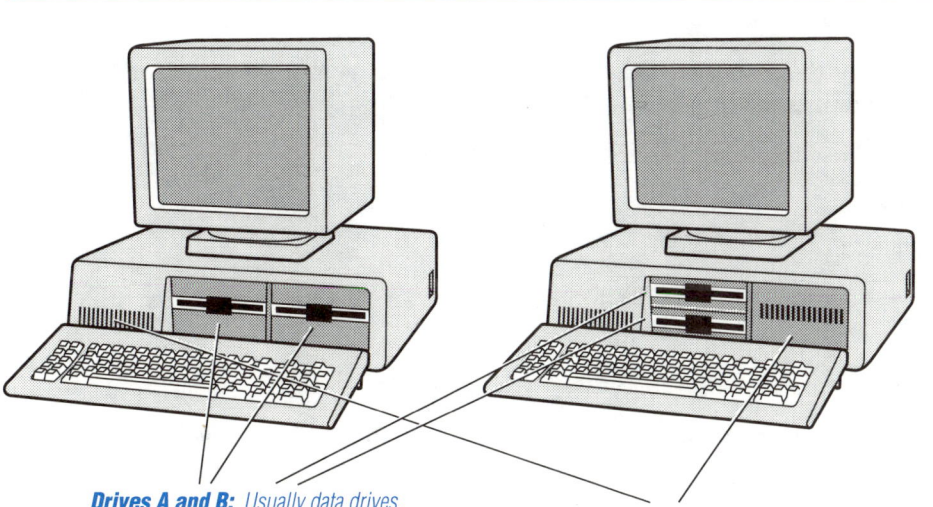

Figure 1.4
Two diskette and hard disk system. Allows great flexibility in file transfer, particularly if the diskette drives read and write two different formats (see Appendix A).

Drives A and B: Usually data drives.
Drive C: Usually the system drive.

> # EXPLORING DOS
>
> 1. How many disk drives does your computer system use?
> 2. Does it have a drive A?
> 3. Does it have a drive B?
> 4. Does it have a drive C?
> 5. Which disk drive is the system drive?
> 6. Which disk drives are the data drives?

MICROCOMPUTER START-UP PROCEDURES

If your computer system does not have a hard disk, your start-up procedures include the following:

With 5-1/4 inch floppy disks

- Open the system drive latch.
- Position the disk with the label on top and the write-protect notch (see Appendix A) to the left.
- Gently push the DOS disk in the system drive until it stops and will not go further without force.
- Close the drive latch.

With 3-1/2 inch diskettes

- Position the disk with the label on top and the write-protect switch (see Appendix A) to the left.
- Crisply push the DOS disk in the system drive until it locks in place.

You are now ready to turn on the microcomputer. The ON/OFF switch may be found on the right side of the computer near the back, on the back, or on the front right side (see figure 1.5).

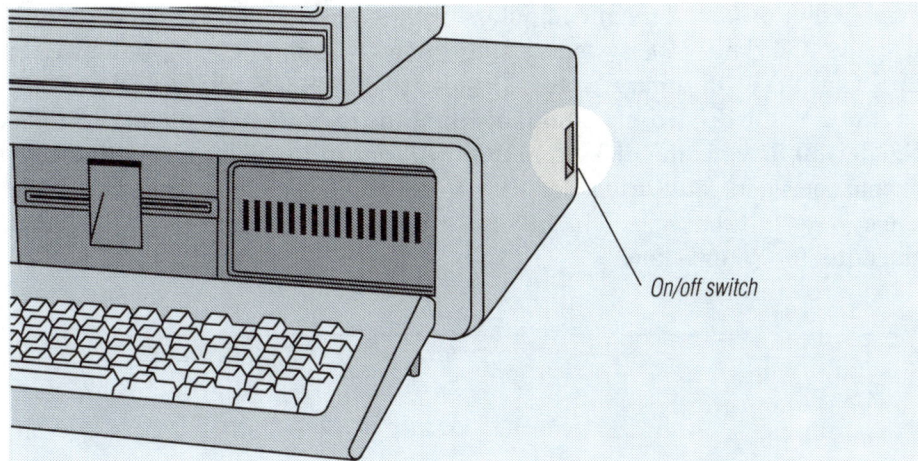

Figure 1.5
Typical position of computer's on/off switch. Exact location may be different on your system.

Finally, if the screen does not turn on with the computer, turn on the screen. The ON/OFF switch is usually on the right side of the screen near the bottom. The screen should display:

```
Current date is day mm-dd-yy
Enter new date (mm-dd-yy):_ ↵
           Change date or press Enter key.
```

```
Current date is day mm-dd-yy
Enter new date (mm-dd-yy):
Current time is hh:mm:ss
Enter new time:_ ↵         ← Change date or press Enter key.
C>                         ← Drive designation will vary among systems.
```

After entering the date and time the booting process is complete. The system now displays the letter associated with the system drive followed by a >

symbol. For example, microcomputers using drive A as the system drive will display **A>**. Hard disk systems using drive C display **C>**. This display is known as the ***DOS prompt***. It tells the user that DOS is ready for instructions. In addition, the drive designation identifies the ***default drive***. In other words, the default drive is the disk drive DOS will use unless instructed otherwise. To change the default drive, enter the letter of the drive you wish to become the new default setting, and immediately follow it with a colon (:). Then press the Enter (or Return) key.

To change the default drive from drive C to drive A.

```
C>A: ↵
A>
```

DOS MESSAGES

BOOTING YOUR MICROCOMPUTER

Unexpected Activities

Nothing happens after turning on computer.
  Check that screen and computer are plugged in.

Computer reads disk but nothing appears on screen.
  Check screen contrast and brightness. If contrast and/or brightness controls have been turned down, screen appears dark and unreadable.

DOS Message

```
Non-System disk or disk error
Replace and strike any key when ready
```
  DOS disk must be in system drive before turning computer on.

  Hard drive systems should not have a floppy disk in any drive when booting the system.

CHAPTER 1: WHAT IS DOS? 7

EXPLORING DOS

Boot your computer system.

7. Is the date correct?

8. Is the time correct?

9. What letter is displayed before the > symbol?

10. How would you change the DOS prompt to make the data drive the default setting?

CHECKING DOS VERSION NUMBER

Once the microcomputer is operating, you can check the version number of DOS by entering VER. This may be necessary to verify that DOS manuals or other reference materials are written for the version of DOS currently used by your computer.

The VER command produces one of two possible displays, depending on whether you are using MS or PC-DOS.

```
B>ver ↵
MS-DOS Version 3.21
```

To display the version of DOS you are using.

```
B>ver ↵
IBM Personal Computer DOS Version 3.30
```

> **D O S   M E S S A G E S**
>
> **VER**
>
> `Bad command or file name`
> *You misspelled VER.*

EXPLORING DOS

Display the DOS version currently being used by your computer.

11. Are you using MS or PC-DOS?
12. What version of DOS is in use?

DOS COMMANDS AND UTILITY PROGRAMS

The disk operating system performs a wide variety of services for microcomputer users that includes formatting new disks and copying files from one disk to another. These services are often subdivided into two areas: **internal commands** and **external utility programs.** DOS must be available in the system drive to use any of the external utility programs. Internal commands can be executed at any time.

Appendix B lists all the DOS internal commands and external utility programs. FORMAT, for example, is an external utility program. To initialize a new disk, a DOS disk with the FORMAT utility program must be in the system drive.

FORMATTING A NEW (OR OLD) DISKETTE

Before DOS can store any files on a new diskette, it must be formatted. **Formatting**, or **initialization**, is the process by which a disk directory is created for a new diskette after it is divided into tracks and sectors (for more information see Appendix A: Disk Drives and Media).

Formatting a disk enables DOS to know where it can store files and where to find them at a later time. To load and execute the external FORMAT utility program you simply type the word FORMAT (upper/lowercase doesn't matter) followed by drive and switch information. Then press the Enter (Return) key. The general form for the FORMAT utility is as follows:

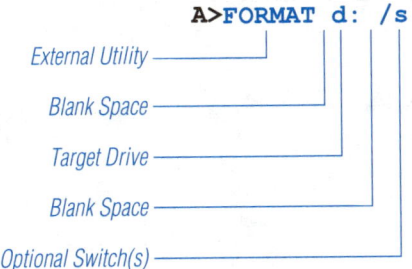

DOS must be available on the system drive to format a new diskette. In addition, the system drive should also be the default drive. DOS can't load and execute the format program if it can't find it. If the default drive and system drive are different, enter the system drive designation, for example A:, before typing FORMAT.

The format program can initialize a disk in any disk drive simply by following the word FORMAT with a blank space and the letter of the drive you wish to format followed by a colon. For instance, **A>FORMAT B:** would load the FORMAT program from drive A and format a disk in drive B.

There are three switches with which you need to be familiar to complete this review of formatting.

/V The "volume" switch enables you to enter an eleven (11) character volume label (an internal label) which is stored on the diskette. It is a good idea to format all new diskettes with a volume label.

/S The "system" switch enables you to copy the three (3) system programs to the newly formatted disk (2 hidden files & COMMAND.COM). Doing this enables users to boot their computer with this new diskette.

/B The "bypass" switch gives you a route around the problem of installing DOS on a formatted disk that contains files. By using this switch, DOS only formats eight sectors per track instead of nine. Thus, it leaves adequate space to install DOS using the SYS command (see DOS Reference Manual) at a later time. The /B switch cannot be used with /S or /V.

The /S and /V switches can be used independently or jointly. Switches follow the drive letter separated by a blank space and do not require a set order.

NOTE: *If you format a disk that contains data, these data will be lost forever!*

The following displays represent some of the most common uses of the FORMAT command and associated switches.

To format a 3-1/2 inch diskette in drive B with a volume label.

```
A>format b: /v ↵
Insert new diskette for drive B:
and strike ENTER when ready
Head:   0 Cylinder:   0
```
Numbers increase as disk is formatted.
```
Formatting...Format Complete
```
This message may vary.
```
Volume label (11 characters, ENTER for none)? ↵
```
Type a name and press Enter key.
```
730112 bytes total disk space
730112 bytes available on disk
Format another (Y/N)?_
```
Type N to stop.

To format a 5-1/4 inch floppy disk in drive A with a system and a volume label.

```
C>format a: /s /v ↵
Insert new diskette for drive A:
and strike ENTER when ready
Head:   0 Cylinder:   0
```
Numbers increase as disk is formatted.
```
Formatting...Format Complete
```
This message may vary.
```
System transferred
Volume label (11 characters, ENTER for none)? ↵
```
Type a name and press Enter key.
```
362496 bytes total disk space
 53248 bytes used by system
309248 bytes available on disk
Format another (Y/N)?_
```
Type N to stop.

```
C>format a: /b ↵
Insert new diskette for drive A:
and strike ENTER when ready
Formatting...Format Complete
```
This message may vary.
```
322560 bytes total disk space
  8704 bytes used by system
313856 bytes available on disk
Format another (Y/N)?_
```
Type N to stop.

To format a 5-1/4 inch disk in drive A, using the bypass (/B) switch to reserve space for system files to be added later.

DOS MESSAGES

FORMAT

Attempted write-protect violation

The disk you are trying to format has a write protect label (switch) in place. Remove the write-protect label or replace the disk.

Disk unsuitable for system disk

There is a bad track on the disk in the area reserved for system files. Use another disk.

Drive letter must be specified

You must specify the drive with the disk you wish to format. NOTE: Only DOS versions 3.2 or later require a drive specification.

Format failure

The disk is not usable.

Parameters not compatible
Format failure

The switch (parameter) /B should not be used with other switches.

Drive not ready

Format Failure

No disk is present in the drive or the disk drive door is open.

Invalid characters in volume label

One or more characters in the volume label are not valid filename characters. See Appendix C for valid filename characters.

Track 0 bad - disk unusable

This disk is flawed and not usable.

nnnn bytes in bad sectors

If this appears in the disk status report remove the disk, reinsert it, and format again. If message persists, you may wish to discontinue use of the disk.

EXPLORING DOS

Format a disk with volume label and system. Enter DOS DISK as a volume label.

13. How many bytes of total disk space is available?

14. How many bytes were used by the system?

15. How many bytes can still be stored on this disk?

CHECKING A DISK'S VOLUME LABEL

Users can check a disk's volume label with the VOL command. For example if VOL B: is entered, DOS will return the volume label found on the disk in drive B. If no drive designation is given, the volume label on the disk in the default drive is displayed.

```
C>vol b: ⏎

Volume in drive B: is XXXXXX

             or

Volume in drive B: has no label
```

To view the volume label of disk in drive B.

```
C>vol ⏎

Volume in drive C: is XXXXXX

             or

Volume in drive C: has no label
```

To view the volume label of disk in default drive.

DOS MESSAGES

VOL

Bad command or file name
  You misspelled VOL.

Invalid drive specification
  You asked for a volume label on a drive that does not exist.

Disk error reading (or writing) drive X:
  This is a device error. Take disk out of disk drive and carefully insert it again. If error persists, backup your disk using the COPY command (in all likelihood, your disk is going bad).

> # E X P L O R I N G   D O S
>
> *Place the system disk in the system drive and data disk in data drive if they are not currently there.*
>
> **16. What volume label is on your system disk?**
>
> **17. What label is on your newly formatted disk?**

DISK DIRECTORIES

The most commonly used DOS command, DIR, lists all the data files and programs stored on disk. The standard format for the internal DIR command looks like this:

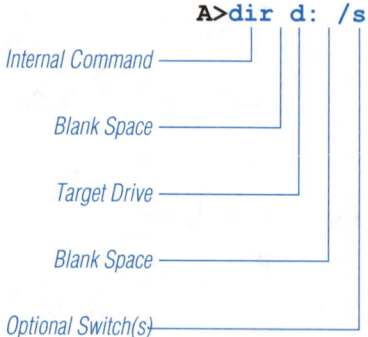

The resulting display identifies each file by name, extension, size in number of bytes (characters), creation date, and creation time. File names can be up to eight letters with the extensions adding three more letters at the end (for more information about file names see Appendix C: DOS Rules for Naming Files and Programs).

If a disk drive is not specified after DIR, DOS will display the disk directory in the default drive. As a result, a listing of the disk directory in drive A: will occur when entering the following:

```
A>dir ↵

Disk in drive A is WORK DISK
Directory of A:\

FOR89-01 RPT      5788     12-18-87     8:45a
        1 File(s)     356708 bytes free
```

To view a directory on the default drive.

The file **FOR89-01.RPT** appears on the disk directory. By examining the disk directory you can see that **FOR89-01.RPT** contains 5,788 characters. It was originally stored on the disk on December 18, 1987 at 8:45 in the morning. In addition, the volume label on this disk is WORK DISK and there are 356,708 bytes (characters) of disk storage still available. On careful examination of the directory listing you will notice that the period (.) is not displayed between the filename and extension.

NOTE: *If you are using a computer system with a hard disk, read the section titled "Referencing Files in a Subdirectory" found in Chapter 5 before continuing.*

Since disk directories can get rather long, there are two switches that help users keep the contents of the disk directory from scrolling off the screen.

/P The "page" switch forces DOS to stop when the directory display fills the screen. The message **Strike a key when ready...** allows users to continue displaying the remaining portions of the directory at their convenience.

/W The "wide" switch forces DOS to eliminate the size, date and time from the directory display. Five file names and extensions appear on each line in order to compress the directory listing.

These switches can be used in combination when a directory in the wide mode scrolls off the screen.

To view a directory with a designation for disk drive B.

```
A>dir b:

Volume in drive B is WORK DISK
Directory of  B:\

FOR89-01 RPT      5788   12-18-87   8:45a
FOR89-02 RPT      9088    1-07-88   2:20p
FOR89-03 RPT      4224    7-23-87   5:58p
FOR89-04 RPT      3584   12-07-87   1:17p
FOR89-05 RPT      5376   12-11-87   1:03p
FOR89-06 RPT      1641    8-14-84   8:00a
FOR89-07 RPT     26880    8-14-84   8:00a

       7 File(s)     301056 bytes free
```

To view a directory with a designation for drive B and using the wide (/W) switch.

```
A>dir b: /w

Volume in drive B is WORK DISK
Directory of  B:\

FOR89-01 RPT    FOR89-02 RPT    FOR89-03 RPT    FOR89-04 RPT    FOR89-05 RPT
FOR89-06 RPT    FOR89-07 RPT

       7 File(s)     301056 bytes free
```

CHAPTER 1: WHAT IS DOS? 17

To view a directory with designation for drive C and page (/P) switch.

```
A>dir c: /p ↵

Volume in drive C is HARD DISK
Directory of  C:\

FORMAT    COM       3629    8-14-84    8:00a
CHKDSK    COM       9275    8-14-84    8:00a
BACKUP    COM       5440    8-14-84    8:00a
RESTORE   COM       5413    8-14-84    8:00a
   .         .        .        .         .
   .         .        .        .         .
   .         .        .        .         .

Strike a key when ready

GRAPHICS  COM       3111    8-14-84    8:00a
RECOVER   COM       4066    8-14-84    8:00a

      31 File(s)   20146176 bytes free
```

Screen 1

Screen 2

D O S   M E S S A G E S

DIR

File allocation table bad, drive X
Abort, Retry, Fail?

This disk may be unusable or you have encountered the 3.2 format incompatibility with DOS 2.x versions. This incompatibility will lock up your disk drive. As a result, you will have to reboot the system to unlock the drive. The problem can be rectified by formatting a blank disk using DOS 3.2 or newer, rebooting the system using your old version of DOS, and copying the files from the old disk to the newly formatted disk.

Not ready error reading (or writing) drive X
Abort, Retry, Fail?

NOTE: *Older DOS versions display: Abort, Retry, Ignore?*

This is a device error. The disk drive door could be open. If not, backup your disk using the COPY command. The disk could be going bad. In cases where this error occurs with several disks, there is a chance your disk drive needs servicing.

Invalid parameter

One or more of the switches (parameters) you entered are unacceptable. Only /P and /W are valid switches with DIR.

Invalid drive specification

You specified a drive that does not exist.

Bad command or file name

You misspelled DIR

File not found

You misspelled the filename or the file does not exist in the specified directory.

EXPLORING DOS

Place the system disk in the system drive and data disk in data drive if they are not currently there.

18. Display the directory of your newly formatted disk. What appears on the screen?

19. Display the directory of your system disk using the wide switch. How many files are on the disk?

CLEARING THE SCREEN

Many microcomputer users utilize the CLS command to clear the screen after listing a disk directory or to get rid of unwanted messages. Using the CLS command does NOT erase the computer's memory, but erases the current display.

```
A>cls ↵
```

To clear the screen (but not memory) with DOS.

DOS MESSAGES

CLS

Bad command or file name
   You misspelled CLS.

EXPLORING DOS

Place the DOS disk in the system drive and display it's directory on the screen.

20. Clear the screen. On which line is the DOS prompt?

BACKING UP FILES WITH THE COPY COMMAND

One of the most versatile DOS commands is COPY. While COPY allows users to perform many operations, at this time it is important to discuss how to backup files and programs from one disk to another.

Informed users realize that it is possible to lose programs and files through operator error, equipment failure, or damage to storage media. Therefore, the

COPY command can help minimize problems by allowing people to transfer files and programs to a second disk. The backup disk can then be stored elsewhere for safekeeping. The general format for the internal COPY command is as follows:

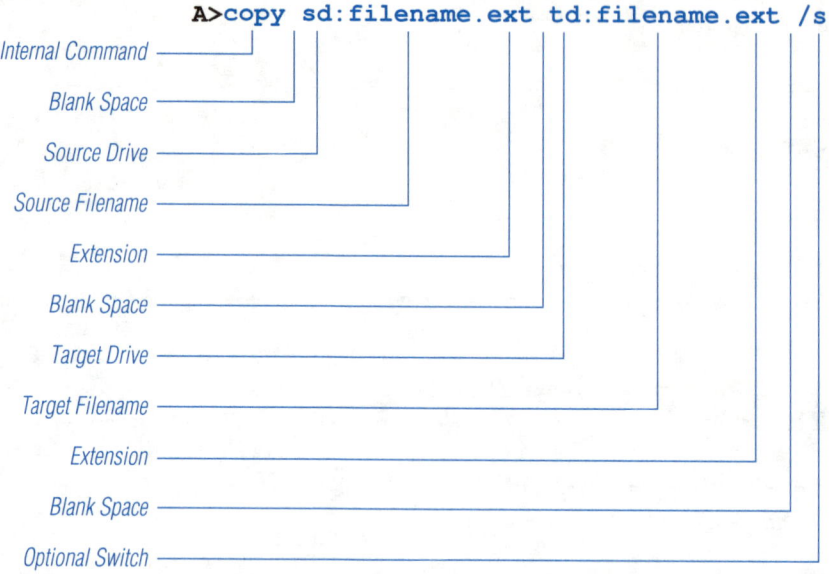

A selected file is copied by identifying the disk drive and file name (*source*) along with the destination (*target*) disk drive. For example, the following COPY command would transfer **ENG1024.RPT** from a source disk in drive A: to the target disk in drive B:

```
C>copy a:eng1024.rpt b:eng1024.rpt
```

If a source drive is not specified, DOS will use the default drive as the source drive. Therefore, in executing the following COPY command DOS will assume that **ENG1024.RPT** is found in drive C:

```
C>copy eng1024.rpt b:eng1024.rpt
```

CHAPTER 1: WHAT IS DOS?

NOTE: *If you want the copy on the target disk to retain the same filename, only designate the target drive. The filename after the target drive designation can be omitted. In this situation, the copied file will automatically keep the name given to the original file.*

Users can change the filename by including a new name after the target drive. As a result, **ENG1024.RPT** is changed to **REPORT.ENG** on the disk in drive B with the following COPY command:

```
C>copy a:eng1024.rpt b:report.eng
```

To double-check that the new file has been copied correctly, users can use the /V switch. The verify (**/V**) switch instructs DOS to check the target file against the original to ensure that both files are duplicates.

```
A>copy c:newyear.let b: ↵
     1 file(s) copied
```
To copy a file from the disk in drive C to drive B, keeping a common filename.

```
A>copy newyear.let b: ↵
     1 file(s) copied
          DOS assumes source file is in default drive A.
```
To copy a file from the default drive A to the target drive B, keeping a common filename.

```
C>copy a:newyear.let b:nylet.bup ↵
     1 file(s) copied
```
To copy a file from the default drive A to the target drive B, changing the filename and extension.

To copy and verify a file from the default drive A to the target drive B, keeping a common filename.

```
A>copy newyear.let b: /v ↵
    1 file(s) copied
```

DOS MESSAGES

COPY

Insufficient disk space

This disk is full and cannot store any more data. Delete unnecessary files from the disk or use another disk.

File creation error

`0 File(s) copied`

DOS was unsuccessful in an attempt to add or replace a filename on the disk. You tried to replace a file that is protected by DOS. Use another filename.

This error also occurs when the disk directory is filled to capacity. Delete unnecessary files or use another disk.

File not found

DOS cannot find the file requested. You may need to indicate the source drive or subdirectory in which it is currently residing (see Chapter 5: Referencing Files in a Subdirectory).

File cannot be copied onto itself

`0 File(s) copied`

Files in a directory must have different names. Use another filename or copy the file to another disk.

Target disk is write protected

Remove the write-protect tab (see Appendix A) or use another disk before trying again.

File allocation table bad, drive X
Abort, Retry, Fail?

This disk may be unusable or you have encountered the 3.2 format incompatibility with DOS 2.x versions. This incompatibility will lock up your disk drive. As a result, you will have to reboot the system to unlock the drive. The problem can be rectified by formatting a blank disk using DOS 3.2 or newer, rebooting the system using your old version of DOS, and copying the files from the old disk to the newly formatted disk.

Invalid parameter

The switch (parameter) you entered is unacceptable. Only the /V switch is valid with the COPY command.

Invalid drive specification

You specified a drive that does not exist.

Bad command or file name

You misspelled COPY, the filename, or requested a filename that does not exist on the specified directory.

Not ready error reading (or writing) drive X
Abort, Retry, Fail?

NOTE: *Older DOS versions display: Abort, Retry, Ignore?*

This is a device error. The disk drive door could be open. If not, backup your disk using the COPY command. The disk could be going bad. In cases where this error occurs with several disks, there is a chance your disk drive needs servicing.

EXPLORING DOS

Place the system disk in the system drive and data disk in data drive if they are not currently there.

21. **Copy ANSI.SYS from the system disk to your data disk. Did the time or date change on the new copy?**

AUTOMATICALLY VERIFYING EVERY COPY

It makes so much sense to use the verify switch when copying files that DOS provides users with the means to automatically verify every disk write operation. The VERIFY command allows users to turn this feature on or off. The general format for the internal VERIFY commands is as follows:

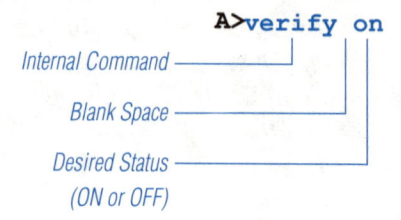

```
A>verify on
```
Internal Command ─────────┘ │ │
Blank Space ──────────────────┘ │
Desired Status ─────────────────┘
(ON or OFF)

By turning VERIFY ON, DOS checks every disk write to make sure it has been performed without error. As you might expect, verification slows down disk output. Most users feel this slight delay is worthwhile since it assures them that files have been written properly to disk.

In addition, the VERIFY command without ON or OFF will display to the user the current status of the VERIFY option.

To turn on verification of all disk write operations.

```
A>verify on ↵
```

To prevent DOS from verifying disk write operations.

```
A>verify off ↵
```

To check the current status of the VERIFY option.

```
A>verify ↵
VERIFY is on
        or
VERIFY is off
```

DOS MESSAGES

VERIFY

`Must specify ON or OFF`
   There is a missing or invalid character after VERIFY.

`Bad command or file name`
   You misspelled VERIFY.

EXPLORING DOS

22. What is the current status of the system's verify option?

23. How would you turn the verify option on if it isn't already on?

PROBLEM SOLVING WITH DOS

This section focuses on problems encountered through incorrect usage of the COPY command. You will find that an incorrect COPY command entry may cause DOS to display a message that is unquestionably an error, such as **Bad command or file name**. In other situations, the standard message **1 File(s) copied** may indicate an error in that the action taken by DOS is not consistent with the user's desired objective. The evaluation or detection of command errors requires both a clear understanding of your specific objective and a knowledge of the instruction's full *syntax* (structure or arrangement).

OBJECTIVE

Use the DOS COPY command to backup a file named SUPPLIER.DTA. This file currently resides on a floppy disk in drive A and it needs to be copied to a formatted data disk in drive B. The full syntax of the copy command used to meet this objective is as follows:

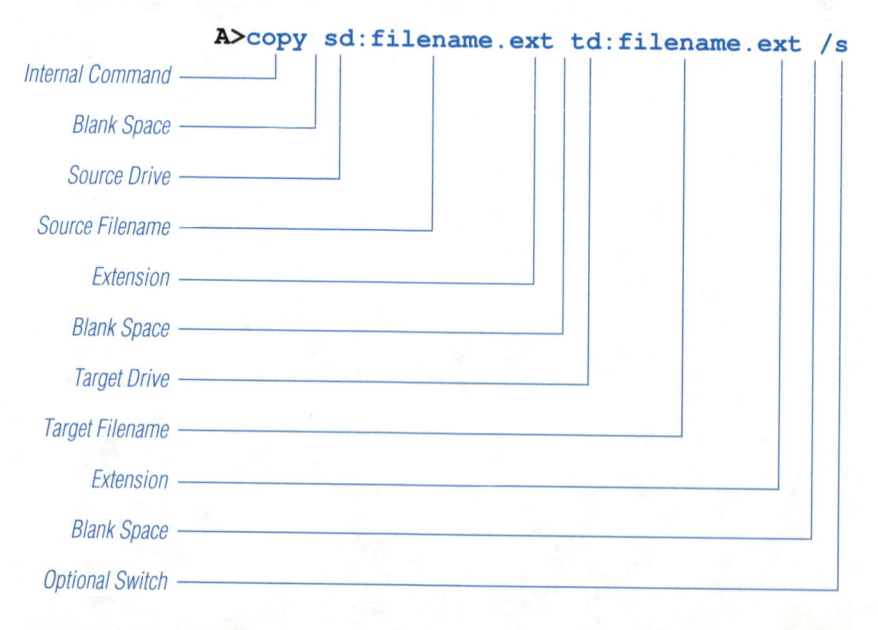

```
A>copy sd:filename.ext td:filename.ext /s
```

- Internal Command
- Blank Space
- Source Drive
- Source Filename
- Extension
- Blank Space
- Target Drive
- Target Filename
- Extension
- Blank Space
- Optional Switch

Each of the following DOS messages was generated by a failure to meet the file backup objective. In each situation you should use your understanding of the objective, instruction syntax, and DOS messages to define exactly what went wrong.

PROBLEM 1

```
A>copy supplier.dta supplier.dta ↵
File cannot be copied onto itself
        0 File(s) copied
```

Answer: The absence of a destination drive resulted in a request to copy the file to itself because the source and target filenames are identical. DOS will not permit two identical filenames on the same disk. So DOS indicates that no files were copied. The original file is still intact.

PROBLEM 2

```
A>copy supplier.dta supplied.dta ↵
        1 File(s) copied
```

Answer: This situation is similar to attempt #1 in that no target drive is indicated. However the target file name has been changed either by accident or on purpose, resulting in a copy of the file under a new name on the default drive.

PROBLEM 3

```
A>copy supplier.dta bsupplier.dta ↵
        1 File(s) copied
```

Answer: Here the **b** in front of the target filename indicates an intention to copy the file to drive B. However, because the drive letter is not followed by a colon (:) the file is actually copied to the default drive under the file name **BSUPPLIE.DTA**.

PROBLEM 4

```
B>cop supplier.dta ↵
Bad command or file name
```

Answer: The copy command was misspelled. This has caused DOS to report that the entry contains either a bad command or the name of a file that does not exist on the default drive.

PROBLEM 5

```
B>copy supplier.dta ↵
SUPPLIER.DTA File not found
        0 File(s) copied
```

Answer: Even though the current default is the desired target drive, there is not a source drive indicated. Thus DOS looks to the default drive and reports that the file is not found and therefore not copied.

PROBLEM 6

```
B>copy a:supplier.dta ↵
Write protect error writing drive B
Abort, Retry, Fail?
```

Answer: The correct command for the objective has been given, but evidently the disk in drive B has a write protect tab in place.

Abort — Remove the tab and re-enter the command.

Retry — Remove tab press the R key.

Fail? — This won't do any good, don't bother with it.

PROBLEM 7

```
A>copy supplier.dta b: /c ↵
Invalid parameter
```

Answer: The command is correct but the switch is not. Most likely, this is a typing error and the desired switch was **/v** to verify the copy.

PROBLEM 8

```
A>copy supplier.dta b: \v ↵
Invalid number of parameters
```

Answer: Here the switch letter is correct, but the wrong slash has been used. DOS thinks this is a second parameter but does not recognize it.

PROBLEM 9

```
A>copy supplier.dta b:\v ↵
        1 File(s) copied
```

Answer: *The file has been copied to drive B as desired but you DO NOT HAVE A VERIFIED COPY. The slash used with the verify switch is still incorrect (should be /v), but because the space between the switch and the destination drive has been eliminated, DOS ignores the invalid characters after the drive designation and makes the copy.*

NOTE: Even though DOS does not require the blank space between the target drive and the switch, you can see that by using the space you improve the detection of errors.

BEST SOLUTION

The suggested short version of the command which would fully meet the objective is as follows:

```
A>copy supplier.dta b: /v

        1 File(s) copied
```

ANSWERS TO EXPLORING DOS QUESTIONS

1. Depends on hardware, usually 1 to 3 disk drives.
2. Depends on hardware, almost every system has an A drive.
3. Depends on hardware, dual floppy drive systems have a B drive.
4. Depends on hardware, this would usually be a hard disk drive.
5. Depends on hardware, usually A or C.
6. Depends on hardware, could be A, B, and/or C.
7. Depends on hardware.
8. Depends on hardware.
9. Depends on hardware, usually A, B, or C.
10. Depends on hardware.
11. Depends on software.
12. Depends on software, could range from 1.0 to 4.1.
13. Depends on hardware, for example 362496 for double density, double-sided 5-1/4 inch floppy disks or 730112 for double density, double-sided 3-1/2 inch diskette.*
14. Depends on DOS version, ranges from 22528 for DOS 2.1 to 53248 for DOS 3.3.*
15. Depends on DOS version and disk size, possible answers range from 339968 for DOS 2.1 to 309248 for DOS 3.3 on a 5-1/4 inch floppy disk or 686080 for DOS 3.2 on a 3-1/2 diskette.*
16. System disks often do not have labels or label identifies the DOS version number.
17. DOS DISK for the disk formatted when EXPLORING DOS earlier.
18. **No files found** is displayed, since it is a newly formatted disk.
19. Depends on DOS version and disk size, could range from 23 files with DOS 2.1 to 54 files with DOS 3.3.*
20. Line 1.
21. Use the DIR command to examine both disk directories. Neither the time nor date are changed when a file is copied.
22. Either ON or OFF.
23. VERIFY ON.

  * These numbers are approximate values.

2
The DOS Keyboard

IN THIS CHAPTER:

Alt

Backspace

Caps Lock

Ctrl

Enter

Esc

F1

F3

Num Lock

PrtSc

Return

Scroll Lock

Shift

Your primary means of interacting with the computer is the keyboard. It is very important that you thoroughly understand its layout and functions. Besides the standard alphanumeric key arrangement you typically see on a typewriter, there are many unique keys that execute special DOS functions. You may wish to refer to Figures 2.1 through 2.4 as you read the following general descriptions.

In most cases, these special keys are a different color (usually gray). The standard typewriter key layout will dominate the center portion of the keyboard. In addition, you will usually find a set of *function keys* and a numeric key pad. The function keys, labeled F1 through F10 or F12 (depending on your keyboard), are located in vertical rows to the extreme left of the keyboard, or in a single horizontal row across the top.

The *numeric keypad,* when available, is found at the extreme right side of the keyboard and includes numbers 0 through 9 plus basic math function keys. Often the numeric key pad will contain an Enter/Return key, which performs the same function as the primary Enter/Return. It is available on the numeric keypad for convenience only. Laptop computer users may find the numeric key pad integrated into the alphanumeric layout.

Figure 2.1
XT style keyboard.

Figure 2.2
AT style keyboard.

CHAPTER 2: THE DOS KEYBOARD   35

Figure 2.3

Enhanced 101-key keyboard.

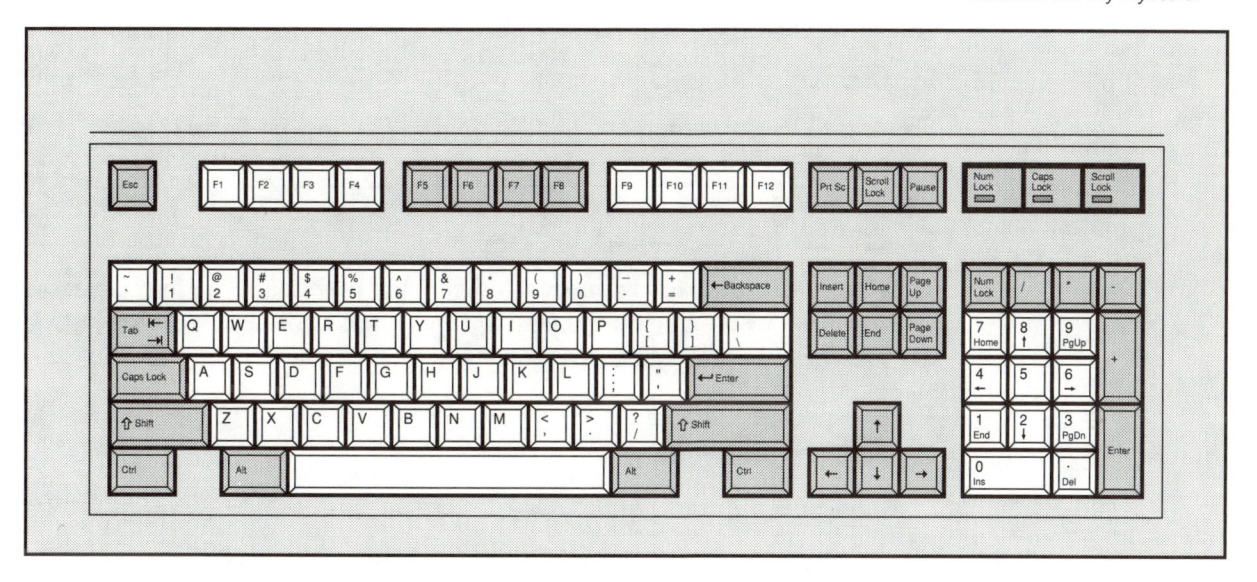

Figure 2.4

Portable keyboard for laptop computer.

COMMONLY USED KEYS

Since there are many different keyboard layouts, it is important that you locate on your keyboard all the keys described on the following pages.

Sending DOS Commands to the Computer (Return or Enter)

[Return ↵]   OR   [Enter]

The Return or Enter key is used to indicate the end of a line. In most cases DOS does not respond to a command until you press this key. Some keyboards use the ↵ symbol instead of the words *Return* or *Enter*.

Cancelling a Command (Esc)

[Esc]

The Esc or Escape key cancels the DOS instruction you have just typed if used prior to pressing the Enter/Return key.

Erasing Mistakes (Backspace or Left Arrow)

[← Back Space]   OR   [←]

Both the Backspace and left arrow keys erase the character to the left of the current cursor location.

EXPLORING DOS

1. Type DIR after the DOS prompt, then press Esc. What happens when you cancel the command using the Escape key?

2. Type DIR /P after the DOS prompt. Before entering the command, how would you change the switch to /W?

KEYS THAT DON'T DO ANYTHING BY THEMSELVES

DOS and many popular application programs use the following keys to activate special features. When using these keys in conjunction with others, it is best to hold down the Control, Alternate, or Shift key first and then press the other key. Undesirable results usually occur if the keys are pressed in the reverse order or if they are pressed and released one at a time.

Control (Ctrl)

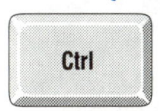

The Control key is always used in conjunction with other keys to access special functions. In Control key applications, you need to hold the Control key down and then press the other desired key.

Alternate (Alt)

Like the Control key, the Alternate key is used in conjunction with other keys to access special functions.

Shift

The Shift key accesses the second function of each key on the keyboard. As with a typewriter, capital letters are obtained by holding down the Shift key and striking a letter key.

Scroll Lock (Break)

The Scroll Lock key sometimes has the word *Break* printed on the front side. Using this key in conjunction with the Control key cancels the command currently being executed. Halting execution, however, is not always guaranteed.

ACTIVATING BUILT-IN FEATURES

Special built-in features are activated through the keyboard. Many keyboards have indicator lights directly on the key or strategically located at the top right corner. These indicator lights are "on" when a particular feature is active.

Numeric Lock (Num Lock)

The Numeric Lock key has two functions. By itself it will activate or deactivate the numeric function of the number key pad on the right side of the keyboard. When used in combination with the Control key it will temporarily halt the displaying of text to the screen. This is very handy if you have text scrolling off the screen. Most keyboards have another key labeled Scroll Lock, but it DOES NOT serve the same purpose. Newer keyboards with the expanded key format have a Pause key which activates this feature in a single keystroke.

Caps Lock

The Caps Lock key has the sole function of locking only the alphabetic keys into their upper-case mode. When this key is active you still can access the lower-case function of the alphabetic keys by using the Shift key. Even with the Caps Lock activated, the Shift key still must be pressed to get the special characters found on the top of numeric and non-alphabetic keys.

EXPLORING DOS

3. If your keyboard has a numeric keypad, activate the Numeric Lock and press every numeric key on the pad. How can you use the numeric keypad to erase these numbers?

4. Activate the Caps Lock and press the a, b, c, 1, 2, and 3 keys. How can you erase the display?

SPECIAL KEY COMBINATIONS

Requiring the user to press a combination of keys is one way of preventing accidental activation of DOS features. While a variety of two-key combinations are used by DOS, only the complete restarting of the computer uses three keys.

Control (Ctrl) + Alternate (Alt) + Delete (Del)

[Ctrl] + [Alt] + [Del] = Warm boot

By holding the Control and Alternate keys down and pressing the Delete key, the computer clears its memory and restarts DOS by a process called a *warm boot*. Basically, this is the same as turning the computer off and back on. The advantage is that the warm boot is much easier on the hardware, especially hard disk drives.

NOTE: *Users with enhanced keyboards can warm boot their system by pressing the Ctrl + Reset keys.*

Control (Ctrl) + Scroll Lock (Break)

[Ctrl] + [Scroll Lock] = Cancel

Using the Control and Scroll Lock keys together cancels the command currently being executed. This result can also be achieved by pressing Ctrl + C in combination. If this does not work, try warm booting the computer with the Control, Alternate and Delete keys.

Shift + Print Screen (Prt Sc)

[Shift] + [Prt Sc] = Print current screen

Pressing the Shift and Print Screen keys at the same time outputs the current contents of the screen on the printer.

Control (Ctrl) + Print Screen (Prt Sc)

[Ctrl] + [Prt Sc] = Start/stop printing all displayed text

Depressing the Control and Print Screen key combination (or Ctrl + P) will cause all subsequent information displayed on the screen to also be printed on the printer. Repeating the combination will terminate the function. Enhanced keyboards have a Print Screen key which performs the same function with a single keystroke.

Using either the Ctrl + PrtSc or Shift + PrtSc features could cause problems if the printer is not connected to the computer or is turned off. Therefore, make sure your printer is turned on and is online before using these key combinations.

NOTE: *The Ctrl + PrtSc and Shift + PrtSc key combinations should be avoided when computer systems share a printer as part of a local area network (see Appendix F).*

Control (Ctrl) + Number Lock (Num Lock)

Ctrl + Num Lock = *Stop scrolling*

Pressing Ctrl and Num Lock keys (or Ctrl + S) will temporarily halt the displaying of text to the screen. Pressing any key on the alphanumeric keyboard restarts the scrolling of text on the screen. Enhanced keyboards with a Pause key accomplish the same task with a single keystroke.

EXPLORING DOS

5. How do you restart the computer without physically turning it off?

6. Use the DIR to display the active disk directory. What DOS key combination would you use to stop the display?

7. How would you print the contents of the active disk directory?

COMMAND ENTRY SHORTCUTS

The following uses of the function keys are especially helpful when slight variations of the same DOS command must be repeated.

Function 1 (F1) or Right Arrow

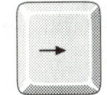

[F1] OR [→]

Using either the F1 or right arrow keys displays the last DOS command one character at a time. To be more accurate, DOS copies one character from the old instruction line to the new instruction line each time either key is pressed. The Insert (Ins) and Delete (Del) keys can be used to add or remove characters as the old instruction line is copied to the current instruction line.

To reuse part of a previously typed command line by using the F1 key.

```
A>copy a:xmas.let b:xmas.bup
```
Type original command line.

```
A>copy a:
```
Press F1 key 7 times to recall first 7 characters from previous command line.

Function 3 (F3)

[F3]

The F3 key will copy any remaining characters from the previous command line to the current command line.

EXPLORING DOS

8. Display the active disk directory. What key would you use to repeat this command?

9. Display the disk directory in drive A, B, or C. How would use the F1 key to change the drive designation?

PROBLEM SOLVING WITH DOS

Since the keyboard is the primary input device of your computer, it is probably accurate to say that 90% of all problems originate at the keyboard. For the most part, this is due to two user-related factors. The most common problem is typographical and syntax errors. Running an increasingly strong second, however, is the lack of familiarity with the command structure of DOS and other software as well. Keyboard problems, as other DOS problems, can be separated into the two primary types discussed in the preface:

- Efficiency problems. For example, using the Shift + Print Screen key combination in conjunction with the DIR /P command to get a hardcopy of a multiple screen directory listing, instead of using the more efficient Control + Print Screen option.

- Recovery problems. For instance, identifying that the lack of response to the Shift + Print Screen key combination is because the printer is off-line.

The following examples will focus on a variety of commonly experienced keyboard problems.

PROBLEM 1

You start your computer and experience a problem. Either the keyboard does not respond or your screen displays a keyboard-related error message.

Answer: *It is very possible that the keyboard connection to the computer is loose or disconnected. Though physical problems do occur with hardware, unless there has been an accident such as dropping the keyboard, this is unlikely. Physically turn off the computer, check the connection, and restart the computer.*

PROBLEM 2

In the process of executing a command, the printer begins to print. Inspection of the hardcopy reveals that it is a duplicate of the screen output. You are well aware that you have NOT toggled the screen display to the printer with either the Shift + Print Screen or Control + Print Screen key combinations.

Answer: You most likely have pressed the Control + P keys. This key combination also activates the echoing of screen output to the printer. Because of keyboard differences, DOS may accommodate alternate ways to activate key features. You can turn off the dual-echoing feature by repeating the Control + Print Screen or Control + P key combination.

PROBLEM 3

You have just entered a lengthy DOS command such as `COPY A:OLDFILE.001 B:NEWFILE.01A` and wish to recall the command with the right-arrow key (functions the same as the F1 key) only to discover that you now have a string of sixes (`666666666666`) across your screen.

Answer: You have activated the Num Lock feature of your keyboard, which deactivates the numeric keypad's cursor control and activates its numeric function; hence the `66666`. First, erase the sixes with the left-arrow or backspace key, or press the Escape key. In both cases, the previously executed command remains in the old command line. To recall the command you can either press the Num Lock key to reactivate cursor control on the numeric keypad, use the F1 function key, or hold down the Shift key to activate the numeric pad's cursor control feature as a second function.

PROBLEM 4

Having activated the Caps Lock function, you discover that you are not getting the shifted character of the numeric keys across the top of your keyboard. For example, the 5 key does not yield the percent sign (`%`) without holding the Shift key down.

Answer: One of the major differences between the computer keyboard and a typewriter keyboard is the effect the Caps Lock key has on the numeric keys. Unlike what happens on a typewriter keyboard, using the Caps Lock key on a computer keyboard only affects the alphabetic keys. You still need to hold down the Shift key to enter a special character associated with the top of a non-alphabetic key.

PROBLEM 5

After the completion of a DOS command a string of unwanted characters or a series of empty returns appears on your screen. It is even possible that a `Bad command or filename` error appears.

```
A>cccccccccccccc
             or
A>
A>
             or
A>cccccccc
Bad command or file name
A>
```

Answer: *The computer accepts and stores approximately 15 new characters in a temporary memory area called a buffer while it is executing a DOS function. Because of this, any inadvertent keyboard entries that happen during another DOS activity is saved and then displayed or executed upon completion of that activity. For example, if you accidentally press the c key while DOS is displaying a disk directory, a row of characters (*cccccccc*) will appear on the screen after the directory is displayed. Accidentally pressing the Return key would enter* cccccccc *as a command. This action would result in the* Bad command or file name *DOS message.*

ANSWERS TO EXPLORING DOS QUESTIONS

1. Use the Esc key and the cursor jumps to the next line. The prompt is not displayed again.

2. Use either the Backspace or left arrow key to erase P, then type W.

3. Hold the Shift key down while pressing the left arrow key or deactivate the Numeric Lock and use the left arrow key. Either method erases the numbers.

4. Use the Esc key to cancel it or the Backspace (left arrow) key to erase the line.

5. Warm boot computer using Control, Alternate and Delete keys in combination.

6. Two answers are acceptable:

    1) Use Control + Scroll Lock (or Ctrl + C) to cancel the command.

    2) Control + Num Lock (or Ctrl + S or Pause key on enhanced keyboards) to halt the display.

7. Two answers are acceptable:

    1) Short directories can be displayed on the screen, then Shift + Print Screen (or press the Print Screen key on enhanced keyboards).

    2) Add the printer as an output device with Control + Print Screen, then use the DIR command to print the directory.

8. Use the F3 key.

9. Use the F1 key to display DIR , then enter the new drive designation, i.e., A: or C:.

3 *Updating*

IN THIS CHAPTER:

DATE
DEL
ERASE
LABEL
RENAME
TIME

Once a system is up and running, computer users are constantly updating (adding, changing, and deleting) data. The DOS commands described in this chapter update disk files or data in the computer's memory.

CHANGING THE SYSTEM'S DATE

One aspect of most start-up procedures is the verification of the system's date and time. If your computer system does not maintain the current date and time, you need to set them as part of the start-up process. Some computers retain the date and time by using a rechargeable battery. As you might expect, one sure sign that this battery needs to be replaced occurs when your computer system forgets the date and time when it is started up.

The system date can be changed by entering DATE at the DOS prompt. The system will then ask you to enter the date in a MM-DD-YY format, where MM (month), DD (day), and YY (year) are two-digit numbers. Pressing the Enter key maintains the current date.

```
A>date ↵


Current date is day 01-01-80
Enter new date (mm-dd-yy):_
```

To change the system date.

> ### DOS MESSAGES
>
> **DATE**
>
> **Invalid date**
> **Enter new date (mm-dd-yy):**
>
> *You used the wrong date format or unacceptable character(s). DOS expects month, day and year to be separated with a hyphen (-). A slash (/) or period (.) are acceptable since DOS will convert them to a hyphen.*
>
> *You entered an invalid date such as 2-31-88 or a date before 1-1-1980.*

> ### EXPLORING DOS
>
> 1. **Change the system date to 2-4-93. As you change back to the current date, what day of the week is 2-4-93?**

CHANGING THE SYSTEM'S TIME

Resetting the system time works in the same manner as changing the date. By entering TIME after the DOS prompt the user is prompted with HH:MM:SS, where HH (hour), MM (minute), and SS (second) are two-digit numbers. The system time runs on a 24-hour clock. Noon is 12 and midnight is 0 or 24. Pressing the Return key maintains the current time.

To change the system time.

```
A>time ↵

Current time is 00:25:16.45
Enter new time:_
```

> ## D O S M E S S A G E S
>
> **TIME**
>
> `Invalid time`
> `Enter new time:`
>
> *You used the wrong time format or unacceptable character(s). DOS expects the hour, minute, and seconds to be separated by a colon (:). A period (.) is also acceptable since DOS will convert it to a colon.*
>
> *You entered an invalid time such as 9:69 or 25:01.*

> ## E X P L O R I N G   D O S
>
> 2. What would you enter to change the system time to 3:30 pm?

WILD CARD CHARACTERS

Once in a while you will need to copy or delete files with similar names. In these situations **wild card characters** can identify where any character (the wild card) is acceptable in the filename. The `?` is the **single wild card character.** It is position-sensitive in that it is placed within the filename in locations where any character can occur. For instance, filenames like pin, fin, tin, bin, win, gin, and sin can be referenced with `?IN`.

The **global wild card character** is the asterisk (`*`). It is used in place of one or more characters. It, too, is position-sensitive, because DOS ignores any characters between the asterisk and the period preceding the extension. It follows the same rules when used as part of the extension in that any characters after the asterisk are ignored. As a result, DOS reacts the same to `*.LET` and `*89.LET`. The 89 in `*89.LET` is ignored since it follows the asterisk (`*`) and falls before the extension `.LET`. In either case, every filename with a `.LET` extension is referenced whether the filename contains one or eight letters.

Appendix C reviews the basic structure for valid filenames and extensions. Common uses for wild cards are shown in the following examples.

*To display every file on the disk in drive A with a **let** extension, using the global wild card character.*

```
A>dir *.let

Volume in drive A is MARKETING
Directory of  A:\

DIANE      LET      2985    1-06-88    7:49a
LB011189   LET      3276    1-11-89    9:21a
SE012189   LET      6608    1-21-89   11:01a
RH012689   LET      1664    1-26-89    8:59a
ST013089   LET      3854    1-30-89   10:00a
ND020789   LET      4431    2-07-89    7:30a
SS032889   LET      1984    3-28-89    9:45a

        7 File(s)    336896 bytes free
```

*To copy all files with **01** in positions 3 and 4 of the filename and **89** in positions 7 and 8, using the single wild card character.*

```
A>copy ??01??89.let c:

A:LB011189.LET
A:SE012189.LET
A:ST013089.LET
A:RH012689.LET

        4 File(s) copied
```

CHAPTER 3: UPDATING 51

```
A>copy *.* b: ↵

A:FRONT.RPT
A:DIANE.LET
A:LB011189.LET
A:DEMO
A:SE012189.LET
A:TOC.RPT
A:IDX.RPT
A:RH012689.LET
A:ST013089.LET
A:ND020789.LET
A:SS032889.LET
A:TECBRO

    12 File(s) copied
```

To copy the entire contents of the disk in drive A to drive B, using global wildcard characters for filenames and extensions.

EXPLORING DOS

3. How would you use the wild card characters to find out how many files on the DOS disk have a .SYS extension?

ERASING OR DELETING FILES FROM DISK

People new to MS or PC-DOS are often surprised when they realize that DEL and ERASE perform the same function. Both are used to remove files from the disk directory. When doing so, you must identify a file by its name, extension, and disk location (if it is not in the default disk drive). The general form for the DEL and ERASE commands is as follows:

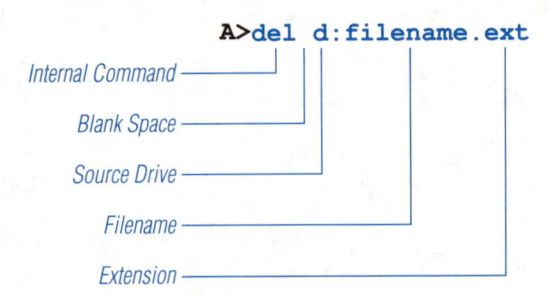

```
A>del d:filename.ext
```
- Internal Command
- Blank Space
- Source Drive
- Filename
- Extension

Once a file has been deleted, it cannot be recovered by any DOS commands. However, commercial software is available that can restore deleted files if the problem is identified before any new files are added to the disk.

NOTE: *To avoid accidentally deleting the wrong file, first use the DIR command to display the files you are going to erase. If everything looks right, type DEL and press the F3 key. This will recall the same filenames from the previous command line.*

The following examples demonstrate common applications for the ERASE and DEL commands. Do not forget that these commands are interchangeable.

To remove a file from drive A.

```
C>del a:oldpaper.doc ↵

C>
```

To remove a file from the default drive.

```
B>del ENG1004.DOC ↵

B>
```

CHAPTER 3: UPDATING

```
A>erase b:*.*  ↵

Are you sure (Y/N)?_
```

To erase the entire contents of the disk in drive B, using global wild card characters for extensions and filenames.

*If the user responds with a **Y** or **y**, the disk is erased; entering **N** or **n** aborts the deletion.*

```
C>del *.doc  ↵

C>
```

To delete every file on the default drive with a .DOC extension, using a global wild card for the filename.

DOS MESSAGES

ERASE or DEL

File not found

You have misspelled the filename or the file does not reside on the default drive or indicated directory. Use DIR to locate and verify the filename's correct spelling.

Are you sure (Y/N)?

You have used the DOS wild card entry *.* for the filename, thus indicating you want to delete every file on the disk.

DOS is checking to make sure you really want to erase all the files.

> ### EXPLORING DOS
>
> **4. Make a copy of ANSI.SYS on your work disk and call it DEMO. Next, erase DEMO from your work disk. What is displayed on the screen immediately after DEMO is deleted?**

RENAMING DISK FILES

For one reason or another, users often find they want to change the name of a file currently on disk. The RENAME command performs this operation simply by entering the command and old filename followed by the new filename. You have the option of using the abbreviation REN instead of RENAME. The drive designation, if used, must precede the old filename. In other words, it is incorrect to use a drive designation before the new filename. The figure below outlines the general structure for the RENAME command:

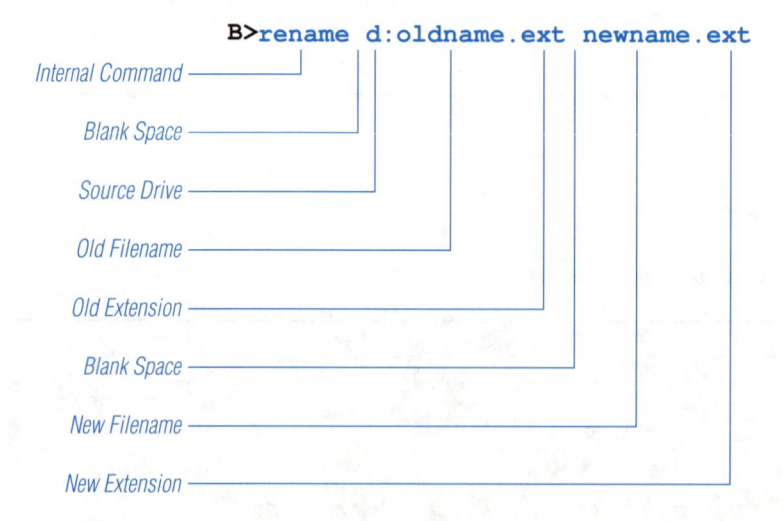

```
B>rename d:oldname.ext newname.ext
```

- Internal Command
- Blank Space
- Source Drive
- Old Filename
- Old Extension
- Blank Space
- New Filename
- New Extension

As a point of interest, trying to use a drive designation for the new file generates an error message. Common applications of RENAME are demonstrated in the following eamples.

```
A>rename c:annual87 annual88 ↵

A>
```

To change the name of a file on drive C.

```
B>ren ybook88 ybook89.doc ↵

B>
```

To change the name of a file on the default drive and add an extension.

D O S   M E S S A G E S

RENAME

Invalid parameter

You attempted to include a drive specification with the new filename. Only the original filename can contain a drive specification.

Duplicate file name or File not found.

The new name you wish to give the file already exists in the disk directory, or DOS can not find the file to be renamed.

Use DIR to locate the file and verify the filename's correct spelling.

EXPLORING DOS

5. Change the extension of the TREE program on your DOS disk from .EXE to .COM or vice versa. Now display the DOS disk's directory using the page switch (/P). Did the time associated with the TREE utility change when you renamed the file?

CHANGING A DISK'S VOLUME LABEL

Volume labels on disks are created during formatting by using the /V switch (see Chapter 1). These labels can be created, changed, or deleted at anytime by using the LABEL utility. Labels contain up to 11 characters. The general format for the LABEL command line looks like this:

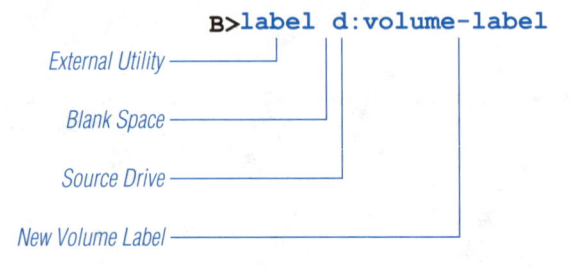

```
B>label d:volume-label
```

- External Utility
- Blank Space
- Source Drive
- New Volume Label

Don't worry about typing in upper- or lower-case letters since labels always appear with capital letters. Special characters like a comma or period are not valid in the volume label. You can display the volume label with the help of the VOL or DIR commands.

It is highly recommended that heavily used office disks or traveling personal disks contain a descriptive volume label. Disks containing software often have volume labels which identify the product. Your name or associated applications are appropriate volume labels for personal disks.

If LABEL is entered with just a drive specification, DOS will display the current label and prompt you for a change. The prompt is bypassed if you enter the new label as part of the instruction line. The following examples show several uses for the LABEL utility.

```
B>label a:MS WORD ↵

B>
```
To change the volume label on the disk in drive A without a prompt.

```
A>label ↵

Volume label (11 characters, ENTER for none)?_
```
The first 11 characters, including spaces, will become the volume label.

To change volume label in default drive using the prompt.

```
C>label a: ↵

Volume in drive A is WORK DISK

Volume label (11 characters, ENTER for none)?_
```
Press the Enter key to remove the current volume label.

To check the volume label on the disk in drive A before removing it.

DOS MESSAGES

LABEL

Bad command or file name.
  You misspelled LABEL or DOS cannot find the LABEL utility program on the default disk drive or active directory.

Invalid drive specification.
> You attempted to change the volume label on a disk drive that physically does not exist, or you failed to include the colon in the drive specification.

`Write protect error writing drive X`
`Abort, Retry, Fail?`
> You tried to change the label on a disk with a write-protect tab in place. Remove the tab and try again.

`Invalid characters in volume label`
`Volume label (11 characters, ENTER for none)?`
> You have attempted to include an unacceptable character, possibly a period (.) or comma (,), in the volume label. See Appendix C for filename rules that also apply to volume labels.

Beep - Beep - Beep - Beep
> The beeps indicate that you are attempting to exceed the eleven character limit of a volume label.

EXPLORING DOS

6. Delete the label on your work disk. What appears in place of the volume label when you display the disk directory?

PROBLEM SOLVING WITH DOS

File maintenance is an important part of computer use. The following problems all relate to the user's need to update a series of files. Initially, the files in the following directory are involved.

```
A>dir b: ↵

Volume in drive B: MAINTENANCE
Directory of  B:\

MAINT001 MEO      1765   1-1-80   3:27a
MAINT001 BAK      1765   1-1-80   3:29a
MAINT002 MEO       988   1-1-80   5:45a
MAINT002 BAK       988   1-1-80   5:46a
MAINT003 MEO      2346   1-1-80   7:32a
MAINT003 BAK      2346   1-1-80   7:34a
MAINT004 MEO       367   1-1-80   2:07a
MAINT004 BAK       367   1-1-80   2:10a
ANLRPT01 DOC      1122   1-1-80   3:33a
ANLRPT01 BAK      1122   1-1-80   3:35a
ANLRPT02 DOC      2050   1-1-80   4:21a
ANLRPT02 BAK      2050   1-1-80   4:24a
ANLRPT03 DOC      4891   1-1-80   6:27a
ANLRPT03 BAK      4891   1-1-80   6:31a
ANLRPT04 DOC      6634   1-1-80   3:55a
ANLRPT04 BAK      6634   1-1-80   3:58a
ANLRPT05 DOC      8554   1-1-80   4:11a
ANLRPT05 BAK      8554   1-1-80   4:13a

       14 File(s)     305062 bytes free
```

PROBLEM 1

This user would like to identify all the memos to maintenance that were written in April of the current year. Memo files have a `.MEO` extension. Unfortunately the creation dates in the directory are of little help since they all contain the same date, 1-1-1980.

Fortunately, each memo has the date it was issued within the text of the memo. However, the user will need to load each memo into a word processor to identify that date. What could have been done to avoid this loss of productivity?

Answer: *This user is suffering the consequence of not checking the system date when the system was booted. He or she simply pressed the Return key and accepted the default date (1-1-1980) presented upon start-up of the computer. Had the incorrect system date been corrected, files added to the disk directory would have accurately identified the dates the maintenance memos had been created. The little effort it takes to accurately set the system date and time usually pays off in enhanced productivity of file management tasks.*

NOTE: *Even if your computer has a battery-powered calendar and clock feature, it still pays to confirm its accuracy at start-up.*

PROBLEM 2

What is the problem and solution when the following DOS message appears as you attempt to change a volume label?

```
A>label b: ↵
Bad command or file name
```

Answer: *The label feature of DOS is a utility program. In the example, the DOS disk must be present on the default disk in drive A if you wish to use it to add or change the volume label on a disk.*

PROBLEM 3

Having completed the annual report, you would like to clean up the disk by deleting the earlier work while retaining the final version currently labeled **ANLRPT05.DOC** and **ANLRPT05.BAK**.

The following commands are issued to accomplish the task:

```
A>ren b:anlrpt05.* report88.* ↵

A>del b:*rpt*.* ↵
Are you sure (Y/N)?y ↵

A>dir b: ↵

Volume in drive B: MAINTENANCE
Directory of  B:\

No file found
```

This accidental erasure of the entire disk, including the annual report, is a typical example of how easily a tragedy can occur. Can you identify what took place in each step of the process and where things went wrong?

Answer: *The execution of the rename command was successful and resulted in the two files* **ANLRPT05.DOC** *and* **ANLRPT05.BAK** *being renamed as* **REPORT.DOC** *and* **REPORT.BAK**. *In studying the delete command you can see that the renaming of the final version of the report was done to provide an opportunity to use the wild card feature with the delete command. From the structure of the delete command it appears that the user expected to erase all files with* **RPT** *in filename positions 4, 5, and 6. The DOS response of* **Are you sure (Y/N)?** *should have tipped off the user that trouble was at hand, but this message was ignored. This problem centers on the fact the characters after the global wild card (*) are ignored. As a result* ***RPT*.*** *was interpreted by DOS as* ***.***. *Thus the disk was wiped clean. This interpretation also explains why DOS displayed the* **Are you sure?** *message.*

ANSWERS TO EXPLORING DOS QUESTIONS

1. February 4, 1993 is a Thursday.

2. Using the TIME command, enter 15:30.

3. Use `DIR *.SYS`. Depending on the version of DOS you are using, there are from 1 to 7 files with a .SYS extension.

4. A new DOS prompt is displayed after erasing a file.

5. Neither the time nor date change when you rename a file.

6. `Volume has no label` is displayed when a disk lacks a volume label.

4 Text Output

IN THIS CHAPTER:

COPY CON
COPY PRN
MODE
MORE
PRINT
TYPE

No matter how good your memory or notes, you will frequently need to examine the contents of various files on disk. In this chapter you will review several methods for displaying data on the screen, printing data on a printer, and writing data to a new file. The advantages and disadvantages of each option are discussed to help you make informed decisions about the best approach to use.

DISPLAYING THE CONTENTS OF A FILE

The TYPE command provides an easy, non-destructive way to view a file's contents on your screen. Just key in the TYPE command followed by a valid disk drive designation and filename.

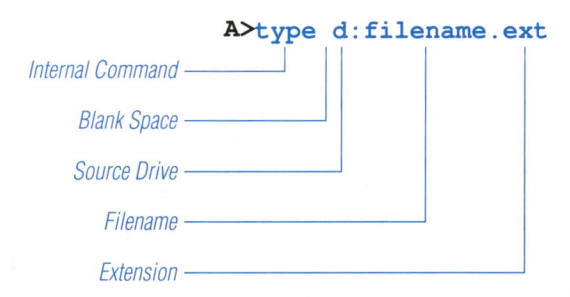

```
A>type d:filename.ext
```

- Internal Command
- Blank Space
- Source Drive
- Filename
- Extension

Having done this, DOS will *scroll* the entire file on the screen. The file is continuously displayed by adding lines to the bottom of the screen, while removing lines from the top. If there are more than 24 lines, the display will scroll at a rate that will defeat even the best speedreaders. Only the last 24 lines will end up on the screen for your leisurely review.

There is also a very good possibility that the displayed characters will not be what you expect. In fact you might receive a serenade of beeps and burps that don't seem to quit. Should the latter occur, you have displayed a file that is not maintained in an *ASCII* (American Standard Code for Information Interchange) format associated with basic text. This will be the case with most program files and often with certain word processing files that contain special formatting codes.

The scrolling problem can be solved with the two-key combination of Ctrl + Num Lock or the Pause key found on extended keyboards. The display can be started again by hitting most any other key (usually Enter). If you do not have the optional Pause key, the required finger dexterity for pressing the Ctrl + Num Lock combination will develop in time.

*To display the contents of the file **autoexec.bat** from the default drive.*

```
A>type autoexec.bat ↵


xxx xxxxxxx xxxxx xxxx xx xxx xxxx xxx
 .    .    .    .   .   .   .   .
 .    .    .    .   .   .   .   .
 .    .    .    .   .   .   .   .
```

The computer will scroll the contents of the entire file on the screen.

*To display the contents of **config.sys** found in drive A.*

```
C>type a:config.sys ↵


xxx xxxxxxx xxxxx xxxx xx xxx xxxx xxx
 .    .    .    .   .   .   .   .
 .    .    .    .   .   .   .   .
 .    .    .    .   .   .   .   .
```

The computer will scroll the contents of the entire file on the screen.

CHAPTER 4: TEXT OUTPUT

DOS MESSAGES

TYPE

`File not found`

> The file you requested does not exist, is not present on the expected drive, or the filename is misspelled. Use the DIR command to locate the file and verify the filename's correct spelling.

`Invalid filename or file not found`

> You most likely misspelled the filename or attempted to use one of the wild card characters in the filename. TYPE does not support wildcards.

EXPLORING DOS

1. Display the contents of the MORE utility program found on the DOS disk. It will be named either MORE.COM or MORE.EXE. What happens?

LIMITING DISPLAYS USING THE MORE FILTER

DOS users have another way to handle the scrolling problem associated with large files and the TYPE command. A special utility program, called the MORE filter, provides the answer. To use the utility you simply follow the filename with a column separator (¦) and MORE. Please note that the column separator (¦) is different from a colon (:). The standard format for MORE is listed on the next page.

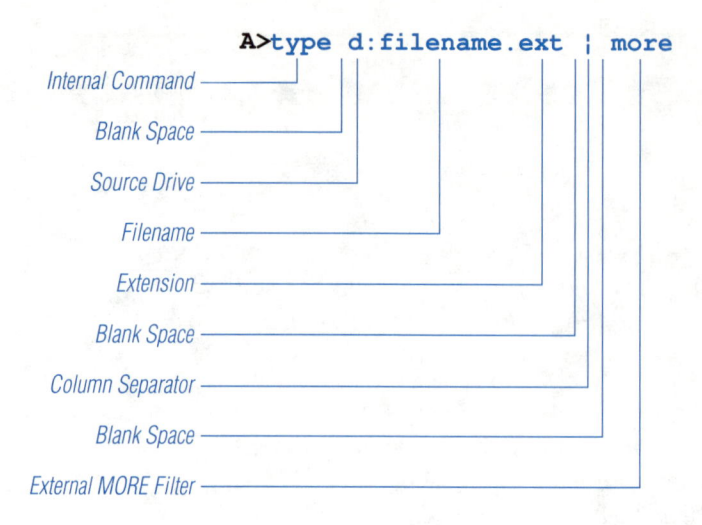

```
                          A>type d:filename.ext ¦ more
       Internal Command ─────────┘     │       │   │  │
          Blank Space ──────────────────┘       │   │  │
         Source Drive ──────────────────────────┘   │  │
            Filename ──────────────────────────────┘   │
           Extension ─────────────────────────────────┘
          Blank Space ─────────────────────────────────┘
       Column Separator ────────────────────────────────┘
          Blank Space ─────────────────────────────────┘
     External MORE Filter ──────────────────────────────┘
```

This new instruction line will cause the output of the TYPE command to be filtered through the MORE utility which will display 24 lines of text to the screen. The 25th line will contain the prompt — **More** — which is the utility's way of prompting you to press any key to get the next screen listing.

Although the MORE filter is effective, it also has two drawbacks. First, it is slow. The primary reason for the slowness is that a temporary file is written to disk. This fact can cause a second problem if your diskette is write protected or does not have enough free space for the temporary file. In these situations you are confronted with the DOS messages **Write protect error** or **Intermediate file error** (see the next DOS Messages box for more detail). Common applications for the MORE utility are demonstrated in the following screen displays.

To display a file's contents using the MORE utility to interrupt scrolling.

```
A>type b:project91.rpt ¦ more  ↵

xxx xxxxxxx xxxxx xxxx xx xxx xxxx xxx
 .    .      .    .    .   .   .    .
 .    .      .    .    .   .   .    .
- More -                                    ← Press any key to continue.
xxx xxxxxxx xxxxx xxxx xx xxx xxxx xxx
 .    .      .    .    .   .   .    .
 .    .      .    .    .   .   .    .
```

The computer will scroll the entire file contents on the screen, 24 lines at a time.

CHAPTER 4: TEXT OUTPUT 67

```
B>type macprop.rpt ¦ a:more ↵


xxx xxxxxxx xxxxx xxxx xx xxx xxxx xxx
  .     .     .    .   .  .   .   .
  .     .     .    .   .  .   .   .
  .     .     .    .   .  .   .   .
— More —                              ← Press any key to continue.
xxx xxxxxxx xxxxx xxxx xx xxx xxxx xxx
  .     .     .    .   .  .   .   .
  .     .     .    .   .  .   .   .
  .     .     .    .   .  .   .   .
```

To display a file's contents using the MORE utility found on the disk in drive A.

The computer will scroll the entire file contents on the screen, 24 lines at a time.

DOS MESSAGES

MORE *(Used with TYPE)*

Bad command or filename

You could have spelled either TYPE or MORE incorrectly. Other possibilities are that you neglected to tell DOS where to find the MORE utility program or the program is not on the default disk.

Write protect error writing drive X
Abort, Retry, Fail?

NOTE: *Older DOS versions display: Abort, Retry, Ignore?*

The disk with the file you are attempting to display has a write protect tab in place. Though this isn't a problem for the TYPE command, it is for MORE since it writes a temporary file to the disk to facilitate screen paging. Press the A key to abort the instruction, remove write-protect tab, and try again. If you do not want to remove the write-protect tab, use TYPE to display the file and Ctrl + Num Lock to pause the display.

> **Intermediate file error during pipe**
> DOS is unable to find adequate disk space for the temporary file the MORE utility writes to disk. You will need to delete unnecessary files or copy the file to a disk with more unused space before using the MORE filter again.

EXPLORING DOS

2. Display a rather long text file using the TYPE command and MORE utility. What does your More prompt look like?

ADDITIONAL COPY APPLICATIONS

Another way to display a file's contents is with the versatile COPY command. The process is very direct since the COPY command does exactly what you would expect—it copies information (data) to a designated location. Most often the destination is a disk drive, which serves as a storage device. Understanding that any output or storage device can be used as the destination is the key to utilizing the COPY command to generate a screen display of a file's contents.

DOS considers the screen an output device. This device is referenced via the reserved word CON. In the same fashion, the printer is also a device referenced by the reserved word PRN. The following format can be used to display data on the screen with the COPY command:

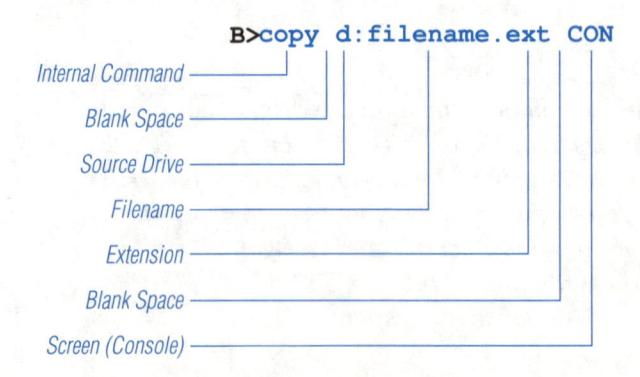

```
B>copy d:filename.ext CON
```

- Internal Command
- Blank Space
- Source Drive
- Filename
- Extension
- Blank Space
- Screen (Console)

CHAPTER 4: TEXT OUTPUT

As with other variations of the COPY command, wild card characters can be employed. However, COPY cannot direct output through the MORE filter. Listed below are some of the most common applications for this use of the COPY command.

To display the contents of a specific file on the screen (CON).

```
A>copy grandma.let CON ↵

xxx xxxxxxx xxxxx xxxx xx xxx xxxx xxx
 .     .      .    .   .   .   .    .
 .     .      .    .   .   .   .    .
 .     .      .    .   .   .   .    .
```

The computer will scroll the contents of the file on the screen.

To display multiple files on the screen.

```
A>copy *.doc CON ↵

FILE1.DOC

xxx xxxxxxx xxxxx xxxx xx xxx xxxx xxx
 .     .      .    .   .   .   .    .
 .     .      .    .   .   .   .    .
 .     .      .    .   .   .   .    .

FILE2.DOC

xxx xxxxxxx xxxxx xxxx xx xxx xxxx xxx
 .     .      .    .   .   .   .    .
 .     .      .    .   .   .   .    .
 .     .      .    .   .   .   .    .
```

The computer will scroll the contents of each file on the screen.

*To output the contents of **grandpa.let** to the printer.*

```
A>copy grandpa.let PRN ↵

xxx xxxxxxx xxxxx xxxx xx xxx xxxx xxx
 .    .     .    .   .   .   .    .
 .    .     .    .   .   .   .    .
 .    .     .    .   .   .   .    .
```

The computer will output the file contents on the printer.

The COPY command can also create text files by copying keyboard input to disk. In the earlier examples, CON was used as the target device and therefore represented the screen. When CON is used as the source device, DOS utilizes keyboard input. The following syntax uses COPY CON to create a new file on disk from keyboard input:

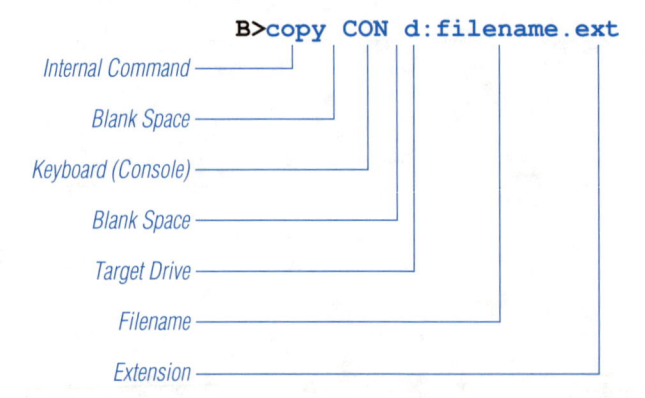

```
B>copy CON d:filename.ext
```

- Internal Command — `copy`
- Blank Space
- Keyboard (Console) — `CON`
- Blank Space
- Target Drive — `d:`
- Filename — `filename`
- Extension — `.ext`

After entering the COPY CON instruction, type the data you wish to include in the new disk file. Be careful to check each line for errors before pressing the Enter key. Once data is entered, you cannot make corrections. When you are finished with data entry, press the F6 function key (or Ctrl + Z key combination) and the Enter key to mark the end of the file. DOS will display **1 file(s) copied** and return the DOS prompt. If you do not catch a mistake in time, finish entering the data and use a word processing program or EDLIN, the line editor that comes with DOS (see DOS Reference Manual), to correct the error.

Another disadvantage to using COPY CON in this way occurs when you get any failure in writing the file to disk. In this situation, the data is lost and must be entered again. You can cancel the COPY CON instruction at any time during file creation by pressing the Ctrl + Break or Ctrl + C key combinations.

CHAPTER 4: TEXT OUTPUT

```
A>copy con b:mail.txt ↵
Joe Shmoe ↵
1634 Someplace Else Ave. ↵
Newago ↵
Michigan ↵
(616) 555-8693 ↵
^Z ↵
```

To create a new file by copying keyboard entries to disk.

*Pressing the F6 key or Ctrl + Z key combination and then the Enter key writes the file **mail.txt** to disk in drive B.*

D O S   M E S S A G E S

COPY

X:\filename.ext File not found

The file you wish to copy to the screen does not exist, is not on the expected drive, or the filename is misspelled. Use DIR to locate file and verify the filename's correct spelling.

No paper error writing device PRN
Abort, Retry, Fail?

NOTE: *Older DOS versions display: Abort, Retry, Ignore?*

This message may mean exactly what it says or you may not have a printer connected to your computer. Assuming there is paper in the printer, the most likely answer is simply that the printer is off-line.

Invalid file name

The filename you entered does not exist or is not present on the expected drive. This error can also occur if you misspelled the filename.

```
Write protect error writing drive B
Abort, Retry, Fail?
```

NOTE: *Older DOS versions display: Abort, Retry, Ignore?*

The disk on which you are attempting to create a file has a write protect tab (switch) in place. Press the A key to abort the instruction, remove write-protection, and try again. If you do not want to remove the write-protection, insert another formatted disk.

```
Insufficient space on disk 0 File(s) copied
```

The disk on which you are attempting to create a file does not have enough free space for the new file. Erase files from the disk or use another disk and re-enter the data.

EXPLORING DOS

3. Use COPY with CON as the input device to create a file called USER.DOC on the work disk you formatted in Chapter 1. The file should contain your name, street address, city, state, zip code, and telephone number. What instruction line did you use to create USER.DOC?

4. Use COPY with CON as the output device to display USER.DOC on the screen. What does DOS display after it is done?

DISPLAYING THE CONTENTS OF A FILE TO THE PRINTER

The simplest way to obtain a **hardcopy** (paper printout) is to utilize one of the PrtSc (print screen) options. These options are discussed in detail as part of Chapter 2. If the file is not long enough to scroll off the screen, use the Shift + PrtSc key combination for a screen dump to the printer. For longer files, use the Ctrl + PrtSc key combination to toggle the printer for redirection of all screen output to the printer. Then simply use the TYPE command. Remember to repeat the Ctrl + PrtSc key combination to turn the redirection feature off. Trouble can be averted if you check that the printer is on-line before utilizing any of the printing options.

The DOS PRINT utility also provides an excellent means for printing the contents of one or many files on your printer. In its default state the PRINT utility will maintain a *queue* (waiting list) of up to 10 files for continuous printing. The general format for using the PRINT utility is as follows:

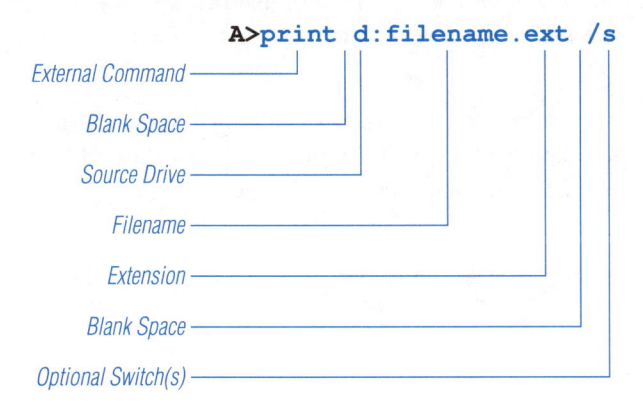

```
A>print d:filename.ext /s
```

- External Command
- Blank Space
- Source Drive
- Filename
- Extension
- Blank Space
- Optional Switch(s)

When the end of each file in the queue is encountered the utility will advance the paper to the next top of page before continuing with the next file. The PRINT utility also gives you the ability to add and delete files from the queue, expand the size of the queue, or to terminate printing should you desire. These features are accessed through four special PRINT utility switches.

/P The "print" switch identifies new files to be added to the print queue. The preceding file and all subsequent files listed in the command line are added to the print queue.

/C The "cancel" switch identifies files to be removed from the print queue. The preceding file and all subsequent files listed in the instruction line are withdrawn from the print queue.

/T The "terminate" switch stops printer output, displays a cancellation message, and activates the printer's warning signal (if one exists). All files currently in the print queue are removed and a new DOS prompt is displayed.

/Q The "queue size" switch can only be specified the first time the PRINT utility is used after booting your system. This switch changes the number of files the queue can hold in a range from 1 to 32. The default value is 10. To change the default, follow the /Q switch with a colon (:) and the desired queue size. For example, to expand the queue size to 12, the following command line would be used: `print /Q:12`.

NOTE: *Typing PRINT without filenames or switches will result in a display of the files currently in the print queue or the message PRINT queue is empty.*

The PRINT utility makes the assumption that you want to use the primary parallel port (LPT1:) for printing (also referred to as device PRN). The utility will ask you to confirm that this is the device name you wish to utilize the first time you use PRINT. If you wish to use another parallel port (LPT2, LPT3, etc.) or switch to a serial port (COM1, COM2, etc.) you will need to use the MODE utility discussed in the next section. For more information on parallel and serial ports see Appendix D.

Don't hesitate to use your printer frequently, the price of paper is significantly less than the time and productivity you lose by displaying and redisplaying the same data to the screen. The following examples demonstrate common uses of the PRINT utility.

To print a file from drive B on the printer.

```
A>print b:chap4.tst ↵

Name of list device [PRN]:_ ↵
```
This message only appears the first time the PRINT utility is being used. Pressing the Enter key sends output to the default printer attached to parallel port LPT1.
```
Resident part of PRINT installed
```
Only displayed during first use.

To print multiple files from drive C on the printer.

```
A>print c:file1.txt ......c:file10.txt ↵

file1.txt is currently being printed
file2.txt is in queue
      .    .   .   .    .
      .    .   .   .    .
      .    .   .   .    .
file10.txt is in queue
```

```
A>print report89.doc /P report90.doc ⏎

REPORT89.DOC is in queue

REPORT90.DOC is in queue
```

To add two files to the print queue.

```
A>print report90.doc /C ⏎

File REPORT90.DOC canceled by operator
```

To delete a file from the print queue.

```
A>print /T ⏎

PRINT queue is empty.
```

To terminate (stop) printing of all files in the queue.

```
C>print /q:20 ⏎

Name of list device [PRN]:_ ⏎
```
            Press enter to accept default.
```
Resident part of PRINT installed
```

To increase print queue size to 20 items (must be spcified the first time the PRINT utility is used after booting).

DOS MESSAGES

PRINT

Errors on list device indicate that it may be off-line. Please check it.

If you have a printer connected to your computer, it most likely is NOT turned on or is off-line. Remember, the file or files to print have in fact been placed in the queue. To avoid any unexpected outcomes it is best to issue a PRINT /T command to clear the queue prior to turning the printer on or placing it on-line.

PRINT queue is full

The print queue can only hold ten files in its default state. Therefore you must be attempting to overload it. This most commonly happens when you attempt to print a series of files using the wild card feature in the filename. It is possible to expand the number of files the queue will hold using PRINT /Q:, but this is not commonly needed. In this situation, the first 10 files are in the print queue.

Invalid parameter

You have attempted to use a switch with the PRINT command which does not exist. Only /P, /C, /T, and /Q are acceptable.

X:\filename.ext File not in PRINT queue

The file you are attempting to remove from the queue with the cancel switch (/C) is either not present in the queue or has already been printed.

No retry on parallel printer time-out

This message is telling you that DOS will not make more than one attempt to output to the printer when the printer is turned off or is off-line.

CHAPTER 4: TEXT OUTPUT

> **EXPLORING DOS**
>
> 5. Type PRINT and press the Enter key. What happens?

CHANGING MODES WITH WHICH I/O PORTS OPERATE

The MODE utility enables you to redefine the default values used by your computer's parallel and serial ports or screen display. This utility should only be used when you wish to change the default values used by DOS. While the default values are usually adequate for most applications, some of the most common printer options for the MODE utility are as follows:

- Change the default printing port from LPT1: to something else. For example, change default to communication port 1 (COM1:) in a situation where you have a serial printer.
- Change the number of characters printed on each line from the default of 80 to 132 (condensed).
- Change the number of lines printed per inch from the default of 6 to 8.
- Instruct DOS to retry output operations to a printer when the hardware does not respond.

There are two standard formats for DOS statements using the MODE utility in printer-related applications. The first involves changing the characters per line and/or the vertical spacing between lines:

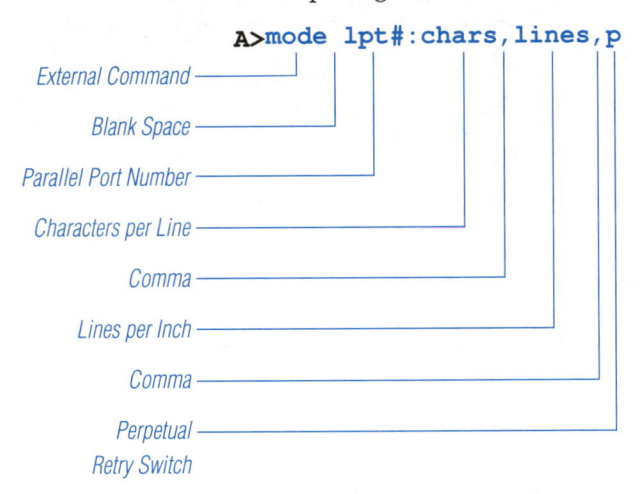

```
A>mode lpt#:chars,lines,p
```

- External Command
- Blank Space
- Parallel Port Number
- Characters per Line
- Comma
- Lines per Inch
- Comma
- Perpetual Retry Switch

The perpetual retry switch forces DOS to continuously try to output data to the printer even when the printer does not respond. This switch provides you with the opportunity to turn the printer on without having to re-enter the instruction. Even though DOS continuously tries to output on the printer, you will still be able to cancel PRINT utility output with PRINT /T. If the intended output was generated by a PrtSc key combination, you must turn on the printer to free the computer or restart the system.

The second format for the MODE utility redirects output to a serial communications port (see Appendix D). The general format for this application is as follows:

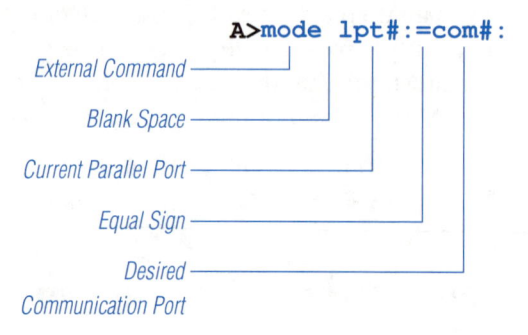

```
A>mode lpt#:=com#:
```

- External Command
- Blank Space
- Current Parallel Port
- Equal Sign
- Desired Communication Port

While this DOS Guide will not cover all possible uses for the MODE utility, you should be aware of the other applications for this versatile program. The MODE utility also changes the display mode of your screen between color and monochrome or between 40 and 80 characters per line. Furthermore, MODE can change data transmission rates and error-checking procedures for your computer's communications adapter, which may be involved with telecommunications. For more information related to the MODE utility see your DOS Reference Manual. Common DOS instruction lines using the MODE utility for printer output are demonstrated below.

To set the line printer to 132 characters per line.

```
A>mode lpt1:132 ↵

LPT1: set for 132,-,-
```

```
A>mode lpt1: ,8 ↵

Set to LPT: -,8,-
```

NOTE: *Older versions of DOS display:*

```
Printer lines per inch set
```

To set the printer spacing to 8 lines per inch.

```
A>mode lpt1:80,6 ↵

Set to LPT1:80,6,-
```

NOTE: *Older versions of DOS display:*

```
LPT1: set for 80
Printer lines per inch set)
```

To set 80 characters per line and 6 lines per inch in one command.

```
A>mode lpt1:=com1: ↵

LPT1: redirected to COM1:
Resident portion of MODE loaded
```

To redirect printer output from LPT1: to COM1: for use with a serial printer.

To return the DOS default from COM1: back to LPT1.

```
A>mode lpt1: ↵

A>
```

DOS MESSAGES

MODE

Illegal device name
 You have not used the correct device name or number within the command line. For example, LPT: or LPTA: are illegal device names.

Printer error *Displayed after a short delay.*
 You do not have the printer connected, turned on, or on-line.

EXPLORING DOS

6. How would you print USER.DOC at 132 characters per line and 8 lines per inch?

PROBLEM SOLVING WITH DOS

Five special, DOS-originated problems are the focus of this problem-solving session. What makes these problems different is the fact that they do not generate DOS error messages. For the average computer user, they can range from annoying to devastating.

PROBLEM 1

You decide to use the TYPE command to display the contents of a letter created with a word processor. As the computer scrolls on the screen with what looks like the letter, you realize it is littered with many strange characters and is not formatted like you remembered.

Answer: The files must have been created by a word processor, such as WordStar or WordPerfect, that does not write a pure ASCII file. The strange characters represent the special formatting notation used by the word processor for editing. Since DOS does not know how to correctly interpret this notation, it displays it's best guess when it lists the text in response to the TYPE command. TYPE is designed to work with ASCII files and anything else will be interpreted in strange ways. For a real treat try this:

```
A>type format.exe ↵
              or
A>type format.com ↵
```

You can stop the screen garbage and serenade of beeps by pressing the Ctrl + Break or Ctrl + C key combination.

PROBLEM 2

You are using the TYPE command to display an ASCII file. Because the file is more than 24 lines long, you are using the Ctrl + C key combination to freeze the display. However, you cannot unfreeze the screen by pressing any key. The only thing that works is pressing the F3 function key which recalls the last command and starts scrolling from the beginning of the file again.

Answer: *You are on the right track with the Ctrl + C, but one key is wrong. The C key serves the same function when used in conjunction with the Control key as the BREAK key. What you want is the Ctrl + Num Lock key combination (or Ctrl + S) which will pause the display mid-scroll and then reactivate (unfreeze) with a keystroke on any other key. If you have a newer expanded keyboard, it most likely has a Pause key which eliminates the need for the Ctrl + S key combination.*

PROBLEM 3

You are using the COPY command to display the contents of a file to the screen. Unfortunately, the file did not appear. In fact your computer is not responding to any logical commands even though you have typed them and pressed return. This is what your screen currently looks like:

```
C>copy con memo0488.003 ↵
dir ↵
type memo0488.003 ↵
cls ↵
```

Answer: *You have mistyped the initial command in the attempt to display the memo onto the screen (CON) with the copy command. In fact what you have done is instruct the computer to copy from the keyboard (also CON) to a file called memo0488.003. Each command you have typed is being saved and would be written to the file when you type the Ctrl + Z key combination or press the F6 function key. If these keys are pressed, you will overwrite the old memo file and lose it. The best action is to use the Ctrl + Scroll Lock (Break) or Ctrl + C key combination to abort the entire process and avoid losing the original file.*

PROBLEM 4

You have a series of nine memo files you wish to print. Therefore you execute the following command using the PRINT utility.

```
A>print memo0488.00? ↵
Name of list device [PRN]:_ ↵
Resident part of PRINT installed

A:\MEMO0488.001 is currently being printed
A:\MEMO0488.002 is in queue
A:\MEMO0488.003 is in queue
A:\MEMO0488.004 is in queue
A:\MEMO0488.005 is in queue
A:\MEMO0488.006 is in queue
A:\MEMO0488.007 is in queue
A:\MEMO0488.008 is in queue
A:\MEMO0488.009 is in queue

A>
```

The printer, however, is not printing.

Answer: *Most likely the printer is not turned on or is off-line. DOS usually displays a device-related error message on the first use of the PRINT utility program. After the first use, it will only print the error message when needed. The files to be printed are still in the print queue. Terminate the request using PRINT /T, turn on the printer, and try again.*

PROBLEM 5

You are executing a TYPE command to view a lengthy ASCII file. Because of the file's length, you are using the MORE filter in conjunction with the TYPE command. You get a display of the file but not the page by page feature the MORE filter should provide.

```
C>type report04.doc \ more ↵


xxx xxxxxxx xxxxx xxxx xx xxx xxxx xxx
 .     .      .     .    .  .   .    .
.     .      .     .    .  .   .    .
 .     .      .     .    .  .   .    .
```
The computer scrolls the entire file contents on the screen without stopping.

Answer: You have inadvertently typed a slash (\) instead of the column separator (¦) between the file name and the MORE filter. As a result DOS does not recognize the filter and simply displays the file in a continuous format.

ANSWERS TO EXPLORING DOS QUESTIONS

1. Several lines of symbols and random characters are displayed since MORE is a utility program written in machine code, not ASCII.

2. Two variations of the More prompt are listed below:

    ....More....

    — More —

3. `COPY CON USER.DOC` ↵

4. DOS displays `1 file(s) copied` and a new DOS prompt.

5. The following DOS messages are displayed:

    `Name of list device [PRN]:`

    `Resident part of PRINT installed`

    `PRINT queue is empty`

6. Use `MODE LPT1:132,8` to convert printer to 132 characters per line and 8 lines per inch. Then `PRINT USER.DOC`.

5
Hard Disk Management

IN THIS CHAPTER:

APPEND
BACKUP
CD
CHDIR
MD
MKDIR
PATH
PROMPT
RD
RESTORE
RMDIR

Different types of organizational problems confront users of floppy disk systems and hard disk systems. The limited storage space on a floppy disk, ranging from 360K to 1.4M, means active users must organize hundreds, if not thousands, of floppy disks. However, programs and data are easily located with the DIR command, since they are almost always stored in the primary disk directory, or root directory. DOS uses a backslash (\) to represent the root directory.

Users with hard disk systems face a different type of storage problem. These microcomputer systems can store from 10 to 120 million characters on a single hard disk, possibly more. Since the root directory can only organize as many as 512 files, users are forced to create alternative directories called *subdirectories.* Here lies the problem. Data and programs can be spread across any number of subdirectories. Without proper forethought to the organization of these subdirectories and their relationship to one another, users can find themselves wasting valuable time looking for misplaced files.

When a hard disk system is properly organized, users will find they can minimize data and program redundancy; create a user- friendly work environment; speed up search, retrieval, and data processing operations; facilitate backup and recovery; and can even help maximize file security and privacy.

Figure 5.1
Subdirectories organized by application.

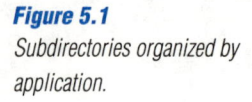

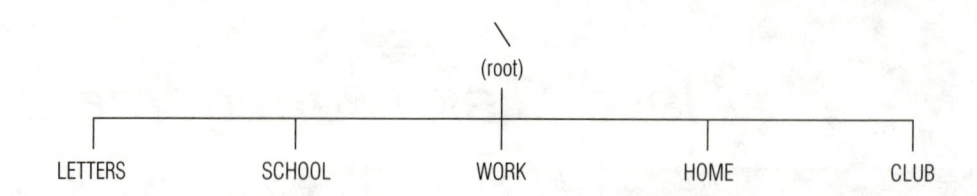

```
                        \
                      (root)
    ┌───────┬──────────┼──────────┬───────┐
  LETTERS  SCHOOL     WORK       HOME    CLUB
```

Figure 5.2
Subdirectories organized by software.

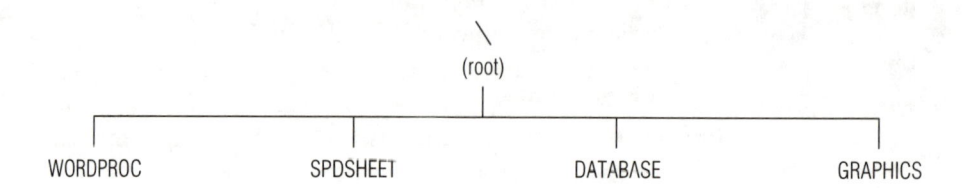

```
                        \
                      (root)
     ┌──────────┬───────────┬──────────┐
  WORDPROC   SPDSHEET    DATABASE   GRAPHICS
```

Therefore, the key to hard disk management is to organize data on disk so it mirrors your work environment. People using their microcomputer as a personal computer system often organize their subdirectories by application or software package, as illustrated in Figures 5.1 and 5.2.

Microcomputers shared by people at home or work can organize the hard disk by user work areas, department, or organizational objectives. Figures 5.3, 5.4, and 5.5 show examples of these organization plans.

Experienced DOS users have found that creating a subdirectory for related data (business correspondence, for example) and another for the associated software (in this case, word processing) facilitates backup and recovery. This organization also simplifies software upgrading. Figure 5.6 shows a hard disk that is organized in this way. First-level subdirectories store applications software while a second level of subdirectories is created to hold related data.

Under this plan, related data files in one subdirectory, such as accounting spreadsheets, can be backed-up with a single global COPY *.* command without copying associated software as well. Time is saved by not copying software that already has an up-to-date backup in the form of the original master disk.

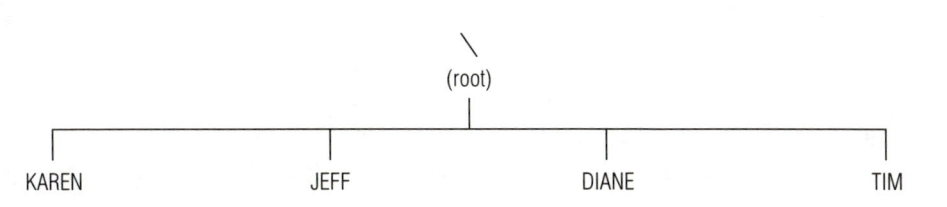

Figure 5.3
Subdirectories organized by users.

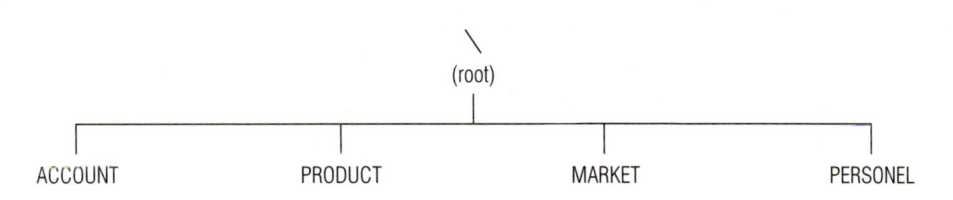

Figure 5.4
Subdirectories organized by department.

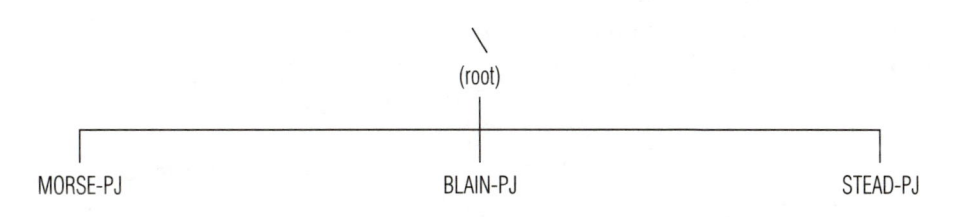

Figure 5.5
Subdirectories organized by organizational objectives.

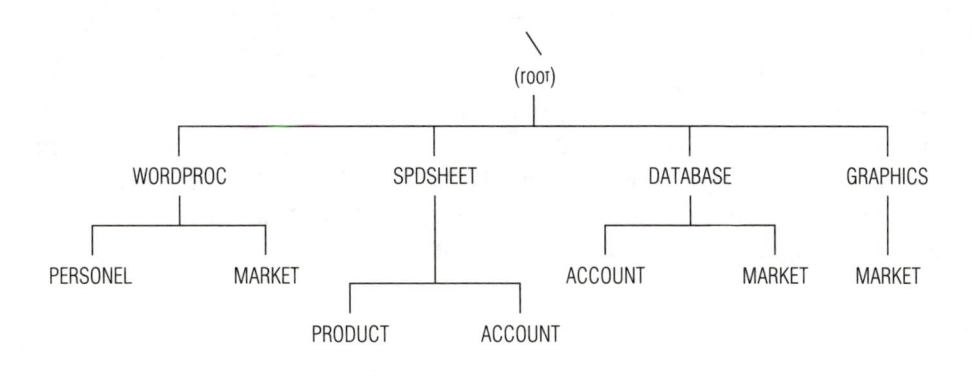

Figure 5.6
Separate subdirectories for software and data.

MAKING SUBDIRECTORIES

A \ (root) directory is created when formatting a new disk. As the term "root" implies, many subdirectory levels can be appended to other directories as shown in the previous figure. Each subdirectory is given its own name when created with the MKDIR command or its acceptable abbreviation—MD. The standard syntax is as follows:

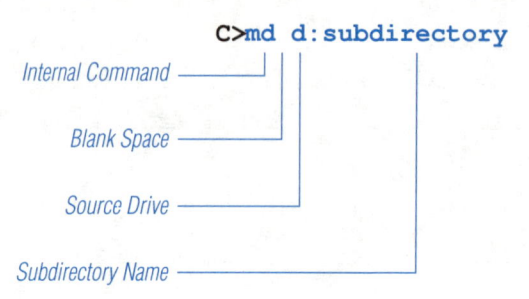

```
C>md d:subdirectory
```

- Internal Command
- Blank Space
- Source Drive
- Subdirectory Name

If a subdirectory is to be subordinate to another subdirectory you must identify this relationship when creating the new subdirectory. The \ symbol is also used to distinguish a subdirectory name from a filename. For example, the following command will create an additional second-level subdirectory \WORDPROC\LETTERS under the first-level subdirectory labeled \WORDPROC (for word processor):

```
C>md \wordproc\letters
```

Characters acceptable in a valid filename are also valid in subdirectory names (see Appendix C: DOS Rules for Naming Files). Two subdirectories on the same disk can have the same name as long as they are subordinate to different subdirectories. For example, in Figure 5.6, "Market" subdirectories exist under both the "Wordproc" and "Database" subdirectories. Furthermore, there is no limit to the number of subdirectories or the number of subdirectory levels other than the practical limits of disk space and the instruction line limit of 63 characters.

Subdirectories are only listed in the directory to which they are subordinate and have a <DIR> displayed after the subdirectory name when listed. The following directory listing of the \WORDPROC subdirectory shows the subordinate subdirectories PERSONEL, MARKET, and LETTERS, as well as data and program files stored within \WORDPROC.

```
C>dir \wordproc ↵

Volume in drive C has no label
Directory of C:\WORDPROC

.              <DIR>         8-19-88    12:39p
..             <DIR>         8-19-88    12:39p
PERSONNEL      <DIR>         8-19-88    12:40p
MARKET         <DIR>         8-19-88    12:40p
LETTERS        <DIR>         8-29-88    11:54a
WP      EXE    223928        12-01-84    1:00p
WP      OVR     10963        12-01-84    1:00p
  .              .              .          .
  .              .              .          .
  .              .              .          .

23 File(s)     17345943 bytes free
```

Two additional subdirectory references are automatically created within any new subdirectory. They are shown above as . <DIR> and .. <DIR>. The two entries reference the current subdirectory (.) and the directory to which it is appended (..).

Common uses for the MD (MKDIR) command are shown in the following screen displays.

```
C>md \graphics ↵

C>
```

To create a new subdirectory subordinate to the root directory.

To create a new second-level subdirectory subordinate to the first-level subdirectory \GRAPHICS.

```
C>mkdir \graphics\draw ↵

C>
```

To create a new subdirectory under the current location in the disk's subdirectory hierarchy.

```
C>md letters ↵

C>
```
If DOS is currently working in the WORDPROC subdirectory, the new subdirectory LETTERS will be subordinate to \WORDPROC.

DOS MESSAGES

MD or MKDIR

Invalid directory

You used an active subdirectory name, or the new subdirectory cannot be placed through the directory path given. Retry command using a different spelling of the subdirectory name after rechecking the desired position in the subdirectory hierarchy.

Unable to create directory

A subdirectory of this name that is subordinate to the designated directory already exists. Figure 5.6 outlines an acceptable situation where separate \MARKET subdirectories are subordinate to both the \WORDPROC and \DATABASE directories. However, the above DOS message would occur if MD \DATABASE\MARKET were entered, because a subdirectory of that name is already subordinate to the \DATABASE directory.

This error may also be caused by using an invalid subdirectory name. The rules that apply to the naming of directories are the same as the rules that apply to naming files. If you are unsure, stick with just alphanumeric characters or review Appendix C.

Invalid number of parameter(s)

This error may also be caused by using an invalid subdirectory name or a typographical error. The rules that apply to the naming of directories are the same as the rules that apply to naming files (see Appendix C).

Invalid parameter

This error may also be caused by using an invalid subdirectory name or typographical error. The rules that apply to the naming of directories are the same as the rules that apply to naming files (see Appendix C).

EXPLORING DOS

Use the MD command to create two subdirectories \DOS and \WORKAREA on your work disk.

1. When you display the disk directory, does DOS include subdirectory listings in the file count?

REFERENCING FILES IN A SUBDIRECTORY

When using the drive designation of a floppy disk, such as B:, you are actually referring to the \ (root) directory of the B drive. Since floppy disks rarely have subdirectories, the drive designation alone references every file on the diskette's root directory. However, a hard disk drive designation alone, such as C:, will not reference the location of every file on the disk. In this case the specific path to the desired file must be clearly identified as part of the DOS instruction. For example, Figure 5.6 shows that files found in the MARKET subdirectory are subordinate to the WORDPROC subdirectory, which is subordinate to the \

(root) directory. To display the contents of a memo file called PARKING.MEM in the \WORDPROC\MARKET subdirectory with the DOS TYPE command, you would use the following instruction:

```
A>type c:\wordproc\market\parking.mem
```

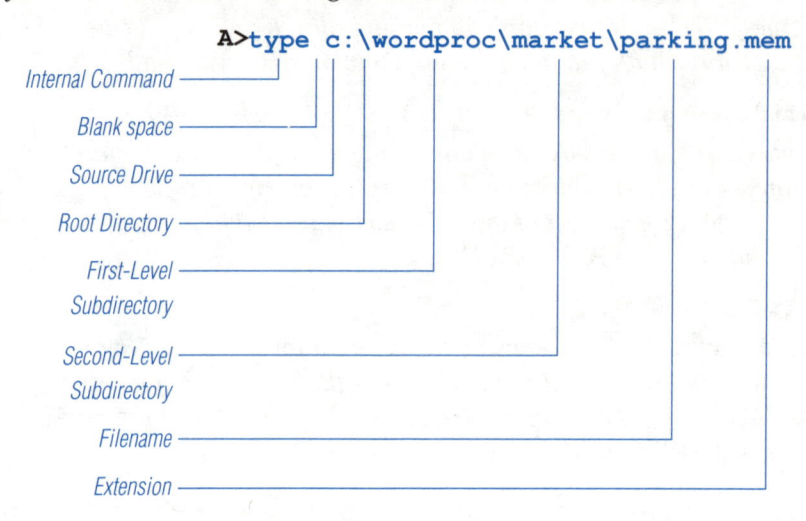

- Internal Command
- Blank space
- Source Drive
- Root Directory
- First-Level Subdirectory
- Second-Level Subdirectory
- Filename
- Extension

As you have seen, DOS assumes files are found in the default directory unless an alternative path is identified. Having to identify a file's specific path can be avoided by creating search paths with the PATH or APPEND command (see sections on Identifying Search Paths and Appending Search Paths for Data Files later in this chapter). When a file is not found in the default directory, the *search path* identifies alternative directories to search and the order in which to search.

CHANGING FROM ONE SUBDIRECTORY TO ANOTHER

The CHDIR or CD command moves you from one directory to another. The general form of the change directory command is as follows:

```
C>cd subdirectory
```

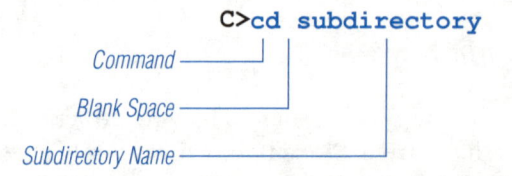

- Command
- Blank Space
- Subdirectory Name

The CD (CHDIR) command can move you up or down the disk's hierarchy of directories one level at a time. If you want to jump to a specific directory, such as the MARKET subdirectory under \WORDPROC, add the path to the desired subdirectory name. In this example you would enter the following:

```
C>cd \wordproc\market
```

Other common uses of the CD command are listed below:

```
C>cd \graphics ↵
C>
```
To change to a first-level directory called \GRAPHICS.

```
C>cd maps ↵
C>
```
To move from the current first-level subdirectory \GRAPHICS to a second-level subdirectory MAPS.

```
C>cd c: ↵
C:\GRAPHICS\MAPS
C>
```
To display the active subdirectory.

```
C>cd \ ↵
C>
```
To move back to the root directory.

```
C>cd \graphics\maps ↵
C>
```
To change from the root directory to the second-level subdirectory MAPS.

To change from second-level subdirectory MAPS back to first-level subdirectory \GRAPHICS.

```
C>cd \graphics ↵

C>
```
or
```
C>cd .. ↵
```
.. is a valid reference to the directory to which MAPS is appended.
```
C>
```

DOS MESSAGES

CD or CHDIR

Invalid directory

You have attempted to change to a subdirectory that does not exist, or you have misspelled the subdirectory name.

Invalid number of parameter(s)

This error may also be caused by using an invalid subdirectory name or a typographical error.

Invalid parameter

This error may also be caused by using an invalid subdirectory name or typographical error.

EXPLORING DOS

Move to the \WORKAREA subdirectory using the CD command. Display the subdirectory's contents on the screen using DIR.

2. How many files are in a new subdirectory?

REMOVING SUBDIRECTORIES FROM DISK

Proper disk management dictates the constant addition and removal of subdirectories as projects or software come into use or become inactive. The RMDIR or RD command removes a subdirectory from the disk's hierarchy of directories. The basic syntax of this command looks like this:

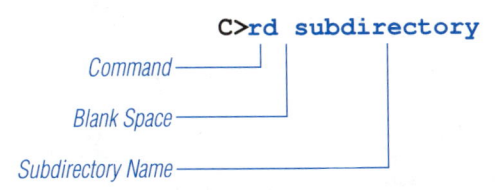

```
C>rd subdirectory
```
- Command
- Blank Space
- Subdirectory Name

A subdirectory must be empty except for the "." and ".." entries before removing it; this means all files and subordinate subdirectories must be deleted or removed. Furthermore, you cannot remove an active subdirectory. Move up to the next level before using the RD or RMDIR command.

NOTE: *You cannot remove the root directory.*

If you cannot remove a directory that appears to be empty and devoid of subordinate directories, there is a possibility that hidden files created by some software packages may exist. Hidden files are not displayed with the DIR command. However, you can usually detect their presence by changing to the subdirectory in question and execute CHKDSK /V. If hidden files exist on this subdirectory, your best alternative is to use commercially available utility programs that are designed to delete this type of file.

Common uses of the RD (RMDIR) command are displayed below.

```
C>dir

Volume in drive C has no label

Directory of C:\DATABASE\DBDATA
.            <DIR>         9-30-88    11:45p
..           <DIR>         9-30-88    11:45p
        2 File(s)     18384105 bytes free
```

To check the directory of the second-level DBDATA subdirectory (to make sure it is empty), change to first-level DATABASE subdirectory, and remove DBDATA from the disk's hierarchy of directories.

```
C>cd .. ↵

C>rd dbdata ↵

C>
```

To remove the empty second-level DBDATA from hard disk's hierarchy of directories while located within the root directory of the disk in drive B.

```
B>rd c:\database\dbdata ↵

B>
```

DOS MESSAGES

RD or RMDIR

Invalid path, not directory or directory not empty

> You have attempted to remove a subdirectory that does not exist or that has not had all of its files deleted. Remember you cannot remove the active subdirectory.

Invalid directory

> You have attempted to remove a subdirectory that does not exist, or you have misspelled the subdirectory name.

Invalid number of parameter(s)

> This error may also be caused by using an invalid subdirectory name or a typographical error.

Invalid parameter

> This error may also be caused by using an invalid subdirectory name or typographical error.

EXPLORING DOS

Display the disk directory of the disk with the \DOS and \WORKAREA subdirectories and note the amount of free space available. Remove \WORKAREA from the disk and display the directory again.

3. **How many bytes of free space was added to the directory when \WORKAREA was removed?**

CUSTOMIZING THE DOS PROMPT

It is possible to create a relatively complex hierarchy of subdirectories. As you can probably imagine, it is easy for even experienced microcomputer users to forget where they are within the hierarchy of subdirectories. Therefore, many hard disk users use the DOS PROMPT command to include the current subdirectory name within the DOS prompt. The PROMPT command can display other information, like the current time or date, within the DOS prompt. Its general form is as follows:

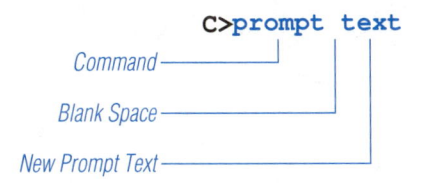

```
C>prompt text
```

- Command
- Blank Space
- New Prompt Text

Information displayed in the prompt line is based on the text that follows the PROMPT command. Here are some of the special alternatives DOS recognizes:

- **$d** Current date
- **$t** Current time
- **$n** Default drive letter
- **$p** Current directory
- **$g** Display > symbol

Other alternatives are listed in the MS and PC DOS manual. If the prompt command is entered without text or special alternatives, DOS changes the prompt back to its default i.e., **C>** or **A>**. To display the current directory followed by the **>** symbol you would enter the following:

C>`prompt $p$g`

The order in which the text or special alternatives appear in the PROMPT command is the order they are displayed in the new DOS prompt. If you are working in the second-level subdirectory TDATA, which is subordinate to SPDSHEET, the DOS prompt created with the above command would now look like this:

`C:\spdsheet\tdata>`

The problem of getting lost within the hierarchy of subdirectories is now solved. A quick look at the DOS prompt tells you the subdirectory with which you are currently working.

NOTE: *The DOS prompt can be automatically customized during start-up by including the PROMPT command within the AUTOEXEC.BAT (see Chapter 7: Customizing Your System).*

Common uses for the PROMPT command are demonstrated in the following examples.

To create a DOS prompt with the current time and > symbol.

```
B>prompt $t$g ↵

14:30:21.84>
```

To include the current date and > symbol within the DOS prompt.

```
A>prompt $d$g ↵

Wed   8-24-1988>
```

CHAPTER 5: HARD DISK MANAGEMENT 99

```
A>prompt ABC Corp.$g ↵

ABC Corp.>
```

To personalize the DOS prompt.

```
C>prompt $p$g ↵

C:\LETTERS>
```

To display the current directory (\LETTER) and > symbol in DOS prompt.

```
C:\letters>prompt ↵

C>
```

To change the DOS prompt back to the default setting.

DOS MESSAGES

PROMPT

&p_

In attempting to change the prompt to include the current path, you used the wrong leading character. The proper first character is **$**. If the **$p** were used, the prompt would display the active directory. Since the **&p** was used in error, DOS displays the text as typed.

> **Nothing Displayed**
> You most likely used a switch character that DOS cannot interpret. In most cases DOS will respond by not displaying any prompt. All keys and commands will still work. To get the default prompt back, simply type PROMPT and press return.

EXPLORING DOS

4. How would you customize the DOS prompt to display your last name?

IDENTIFYING SEARCH PATHS FOR PROGRAMS

One method for organizing a hard disk requires creating one subdirectory for each software package and other subdirectories for related data. However, DOS only works within the currently active subdirectory. So the question arises: How do you work with data in one subdirectory when the software resides in another directory? The answer to this problem rests with the PATH command. This command directs DOS to look at another subdirectory when a program cannot be found on the current directory. The general syntax for the PATH command is as follows:

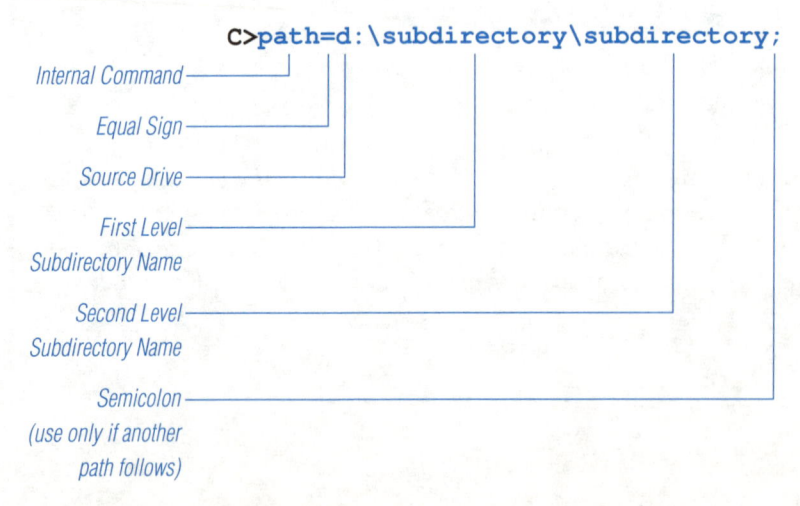

```
C>path=d:\subdirectory\subdirectory;
```

- Internal Command
- Equal Sign
- Source Drive
- First Level Subdirectory Name
- Second Level Subdirectory Name
- Semicolon (use only if another path follows)

For example, to avoid cluttering the hard disk's root directory, experienced DOS users place all the DOS utility programs into a subdirectory, usually called \DOS. The following PATH command is then used to tell DOS to look at \DOS whenever it cannot find the needed utility program in the active directory:

> B>`path=c:\dos`

NOTE: *Entering the PATH command followed by a semicolon (PATH;) nullifies previous PATH commands.*

Several search paths can be established through a single PATH command. In this case, each drive designation and/or subdirectory name must be separated in the instruction line by a semicolon. Do not use blank spaces to separate subdirectory names. DOS will search each directory in the command order until the program it is looking for is found or until every directory in the search path is examined. The following command would establish alternative search paths to a DOS subdirectory (\DOS), word processing subdirectory (\WP), and spelling checker subdirectory (SPELL) which is subordinate to WP:

> C>`path \dos;\wp;\wp\spell`

NOTE: *The active path is displayed by entering PATH without any parameters.*

The PATH command can only be used to find program files that use the .COM, .EXE, or .BAT extensions. Inactive paths will be ignored at the time of execution and errors in the path description are not found until an alternative path needs examination. Several applications for the PATH command are listed below.

```
C>path=\graphics\barchart ↵
C>
```

To set a search path to the BARCHART subdirectory which is subordinate to the \GRAPHICS subdirectory.

```
C>path=a:\;b:\ ↵
C>
```

To set a search path to root directories in drive A and B.

To establish a search path to the first-level \SPDSHEET and \DATABASE subdirectories.

```
C>path=\spdsheet;\database ↵

C>
```

To display the current search path.

```
C>path ↵

PATH=C:\SPDSHEET;\DATABASE
```

To remove the current search path.

```
C>path; ↵

C>
```

DOS MESSAGES

PATH

PATH=:
> In attempting to set the current path back to a NO PATH status the colon (:) was used instead of the semicolon (;). This caused an invalid path to be established. Type PATH; to remove the incorrect path.

Invalid drive in search path
> You have referenced a search path that does not exist on the designated disk drive.

CHAPTER 5: HARD DISK MANAGEMENT 103

> **EXPLORING DOS**
>
> 5. When using PATH, what does DOS display when no active path is available?
>
> 6. What DOS command would you use to establish a search path back to \DOS and \WORKAREA on your workdisk?

APPENDING SEARCH PATHS FOR DATA FILES

With data and programs stored in different subdirectories it is desirable to set alternative search paths for data files. Since the PATH command only works with program files, search paths for data files are specified by the APPEND utility. The general form for the APPEND utility looks like this:

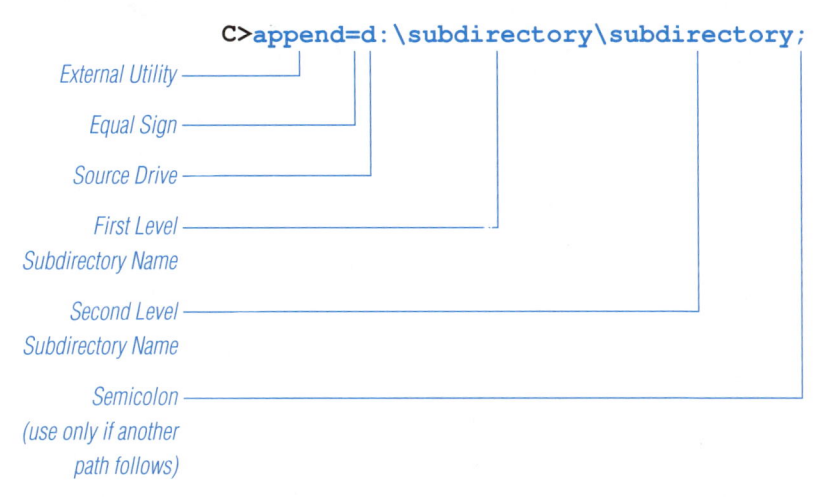

```
C>append=d:\subdirectory\subdirectory;
```

- External Utility
- Equal Sign
- Source Drive
- First Level Subdirectory Name
- Second Level Subdirectory Name
- Semicolon (use only if another path follows)

If you wanted DOS to search the \MISPAPER subdirectory whenever it cannot find a data file on the current subdirectory, then the following command line would achieve this end:

```
C>append=\mispaper
```

NOTE: *Entering APPEND followed by a semicolon (APPEND;) nullifies the previous APPEND instruction.*

Multiple search paths can be established with APPEND. Situations in which you wanted the \LETTERS, \MEMOS, and \PROPOSAL subdirectories searched would employ the following APPEND utility:

C>`append=\letters;\memos;\proposal`

In this case, each subdirectory name must be separated by semicolons and blank spaces cannot occur between subdirectory names. As with the PATH command, directories are searched in the same order they appear in the instruction line. If subdirectories within the search path contain common filenames, DOS will use the first filename it finds that matches the desired filename and extension. References to inactive directories will be ignored at the time of execution and errors in the instruction line are not found until an alternative subdirectory needs examination.

The active path is displayed by entering APPEND without any parameters. Several applications are listed below.

To look for data files in the LECTURES subdirectory, which is subordinate to the \SCHOOL subdirectory.

```
C>append=\school\lectures ↵

C>
```

To search the root directories of the disks in drives A and B for data files.

```
C>append=a:\;b:\ ↵

C>
```

To examine the \SEMINARS and \WORKSHOP subdirectories when data files are not found in the current directory.

```
C>append=\seminars;\workshop ↵

C>
```

CHAPTER 5: HARD DISK MANAGEMENT

```
C>append ↵
APPEND=\SEMINARS;\WORKSHOP
C>
```

To display the current search path for data files.

```
C>append; ↵
C>
```

To remove the current search path for data files.

DOS MESSAGES

APPEND

No appended directories
You forgot to include the subdirectory names you want to use.

Bad command or file name
Your version of DOS does not support the APPEND utility, you misspelled APPEND, or you did not specify the correct path to the external APPEND utility program.

EXPLORING DOS

7. What instruction would make DOS search the \HOMEWORK subdirectory when a file is not found on the current directory?
8. How would you find DOS's current search path for data files?

BACKING UP LARGE DISK FILES

Another problem related to hard disk management is how to backup files that exceed your diskette's storage capacity. The BACKUP utility solves this problem by modifying these files and copying them to as many diskettes as necessary. Files you are backing up have special headers appended to the beginning. Data in these headers correspond to data in the BACKUPID.@@@ file, which is added to the target disk's root directory.

DOS versions 3.3 and newer backup files to a single file named BACKUP.nnn, where nnn is the number of the backup disk. For example, BACKUP.001 is on the first backup disk. A second file named CONTROL.nnn contains all the file and path names for the corresponding BACKUP.nnn file. These two files are the only files which appear on each backup disk. The general format of the BACKUP utility is as follows:

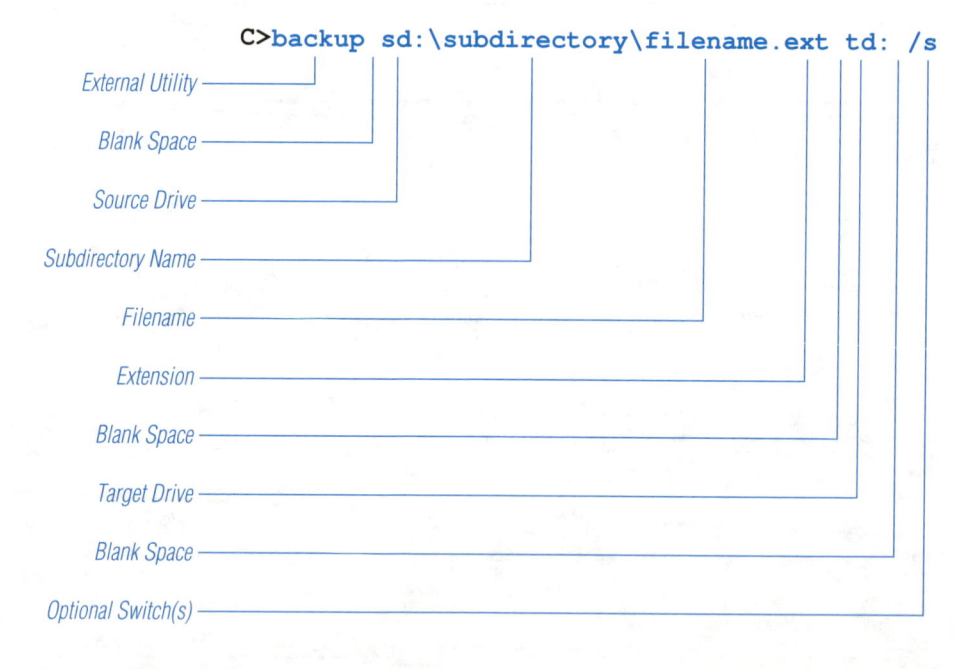

```
C>backup sd:\subdirectory\filename.ext td: /s
```

- External Utility
- Blank Space
- Source Drive
- Subdirectory Name
- Filename
- Extension
- Blank Space
- Target Drive
- Blank Space
- Optional Switch(s)

The BACKUP utility works with any combination of hard and floppy disks, even diskette to diskette backups. However, these appended files should not be used in this format. The RESTORE utility (discussed in the next section) must intercede before a BACKUPed file can be used again. As a result, most DOS users employ the COPY command to backup floppy disk files that do not warrant using the BACKUP utility. Furthermore, copied files are duplicates ready for use and do not contain unusable data headers.

Database, spreadsheet and graphics users often create files sizes of 400K or more. To backup the 432K file VOTERS.DBS in drive C to drive B, the following BACKUP statement would be used:

    C>`backup voters.dbs b:`

If the source disk is a floppy disk, it cannot be copy protected or have the write-protect notch covered since DOS updates file information in the source disk's directory. The target disk must be formatted before executing the BACKUP utility in earlier versions of DOS. Target disks already holding data are erased unless the /A switch is used. When the target disk is a hard disk, the new files are placed in the \BACKUP subdirectory. The root directory is used when the target drive is a floppy disk.

Several switches are available with the BACKUP utility:

/S The "subdirectory" switch tells DOS to include all subordinate subdirectories as part of the backup.

/M The "modify" switch indicates that only files modified since the last backup should be used.

/A The "add" switch allows DOS to add the new backup files to the last backup disk and continues from that point. If this switch is not used, every file currently on the target disk will be erased when the BACKUP utility is executed.

/D The "date" switch indicates that only files modified after the designated date should be used.

/F The "format" switch enables you to use unformatted disks when backing up files. This feature was added to the BACKUP utility in DOS version 3.3. When the /F is included in the instruction line, DOS checks to see if the target disk is formatted. When unformatted disks are encountered, DOS executes the FORMAT utility and initializes the disk prior to continuing the backup currently in progress.

NOTE: *When using the /F switch, DOS must be able to locate FORMAT.COM (or .EXE). This means the FORMAT utility program must be available in the active directory or through the current search path.*

Wildcard characters (`*` and `?`) can be used to backup different file combinations with a single command. When running the BACKUP utility you must stay by your computer and interact with DOS. At one time or another DOS may ask you to insert a disk into the source drive and one or more disks into the target disk drive. The backup of a full, 20M hard disk onto double-sided 9 sector floppy disks could use as many as 50 target disks. The following screen displays demonstrate common applications for the BACKUP utility.

To copy the file CLOWN.PIC on drive C (\GRAPHICS subdirectory) to the disk in drive B.

```
C>backup c:\graphics\clown.pic b: /a

Insert last backup diskette in drive B:
Strike any key when ready.

*** Backing up files to drive B: ***
Diskette Number: 02

\GRAPHICS\CLOWN.PIC

C>
```

To copy every recently changed file in the currently active drive C (MEMOS subdirectory) to drive A, while the other files on the disk in drive A are erased.

```
C>cd \memos

C>backup c:*.* a: /m

Insert backup diskette 01 in drive A:

Warning! Files in the target drive
A:\ root directory will be erased
Strike any key when ready

*** Backing up files to drive A: ***
Diskette Number: 01

\MEMOS\HB1001.MEM
\MEMOS\JS1002.MEM

C>
```

```
C>backup c:\ a: /s ↵

Insert backup diskette 01 in drive A:

Warning! Files in the target drive
A:\ root directory will be erased
Strike any key when ready

*** Backing up files to drive A: ***
Diskette Number: 01

\COMMAND.COM
\ANSI.SYS
    .   .
    .   .
\DOS\FORMAT.EXE
\DOS\BACKUP.EXE


Insert backup diskette 02 in drive A:

Warning! Files in the target drive
A:\ root directory will be erased
Strike any key when ready

*** Backing up files to drive A: ***
Diskette Number: 02

\DOS\BACKUP.EXE
    .   .
    .   .
    .   .
```

To copy the complete contents of the hard disk in drive C to a series of floppy disks in drive A.

Backup continues until every subdirectory is covered.

To copy every file in the currently active directory with a .WKS extension modified since September 23, 1988, to drive B.

```
C>backup c:*.wks b: /a /d:9-23-88 ↵

Insert last backup diskette in drive B:
Strike any key when ready.

*** Backing up files to drive B: ***
Diskette Number: 04

\SPREADSHEET\BUDGET89.WKS

C>
```

To copy the contents of the \ACAD subdirectory on Drive C using the /F switch to format a disk in Drive B.

```
C>backup c:\acad\*.* b: /f ↵

*** Backing up files to drive B: ***
Diskette Number: 01


Warning! Files in the target drive
B:\ root directory will be erased
Strike any key when ready


Head: nn   Cylinder: nn
```
                          Replaced with Format complete.
```
            362496 bytes total disk space
            362496 bytes available on disk


Format another (Y/N)?n ↵


***Backing up files to drive B:
Diskette Number: 01
```

```
\ACAD\ACAD.OVL
\ACAD\ACAD1.MID
\ACAD\ACAD0.OVL
\ACAD\ACAD3.OVL

Insert backup diskette 02 in drive B:

Warning!.....
```
Backup continues.

```
C>dir b: ↵

Volume in drive B is BACKUP    001
Directory of B:\

BACKUP    001    360712   11-05-88    4:50p
CONTROL   001       345   11-05-88    4:50p
        2 File(s)         0 bytes free
```

To display the directory of a DOS VERSION 3.3 backup disk.

DOS MESSAGES

BACKUP

Invalid argument

The argument, usually a switch, in your instruction line is not acceptable. Usually the error is in the date switch when it is used.

Invalid parameter(s)

One of your switches is unacceptable.

Not able to back up (or restore) file
> There is an error in the source or target disk. If the error is with the source disk, you should promptly start the error recovery procedures discussed in Chapter 6.

Target disk cannot be used for backup
> Your target disk is bad. Try reformatting the disk.

Unable to use
> The backup utility cannot remove a file or files on the target disk. The most common cause of this message is due to the presence of READ-ONLY files on the disk. You could use the ATTRIB utility to turn the read-only attribute off (see Chapter 6).

Last backup diskette not inserted
> When using BACKUP with the /A "add" switch DOS appends files starting with the last disk used in the previous back up. Repeat the instruction using another disk and remember to mark the backup disks and store them in the backup sequence.

Cannot execute FORMAT
> When using BACKUP with the /F "format" switch DOS executes the external FORMAT utility program. This messages indicates that DOS cannot find the FORMAT utility.

EXPLORING DOS

Backup FORMAT.COM (or FORMAT.EXE) to your new diskette using the BACKUP utility program. Display the directory of the backup disk.

9. How many bytes of disk space does BACKUP.@@@ or CONTROL.001 reserve?

10. Is the creation time associated with the backup file different from the FORMAT utility found on the original DOS disk?

RESTORING FILES SAVED WITH BACKUP UTILITY

Once files are stored using the BACKUP utility, the RESTORE utility must be executed before using them again. The general structure of a RESTORE statement looks like this:

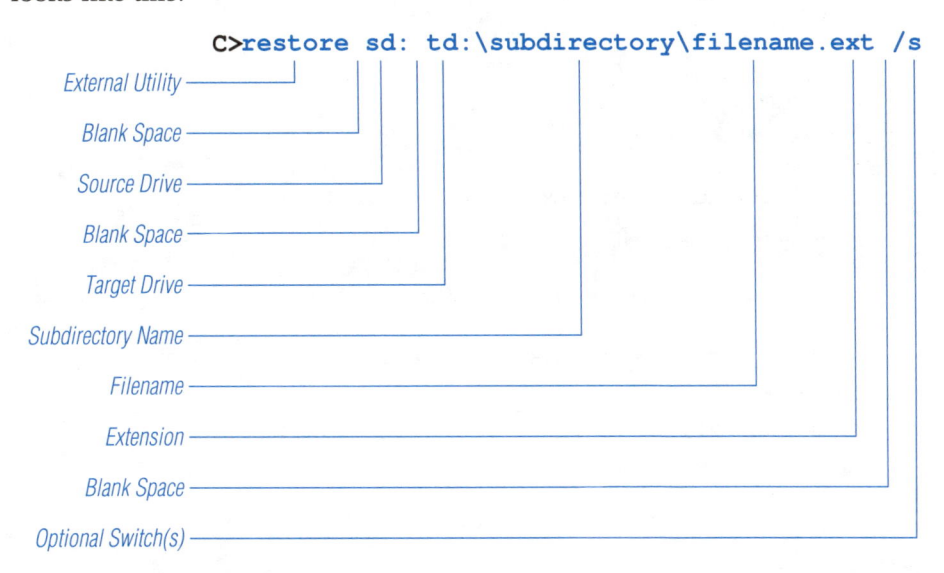

```
C>restore sd: td:\subdirectory\filename.ext /s
```

- External Utility
- Blank Space
- Source Drive
- Blank Space
- Target Drive
- Subdirectory Name
- Filename
- Extension
- Blank Space
- Optional Switch(s)

If an alternative subdirectory is not given as part of the RESTORE statement, files will be restored to the current directory. Files stored on several floppy disks are restored in order, starting from diskette 1. DOS prompts the insertion of source disks as needed. If disks are inserted into the source drive out of sequence the following error message is displayed:

```
Warning! Diskette is out of sequence
Replace diskette or continue if okay
strike any key when ready
```

Two switches are available with the RESTORE utility.

/S The "subdirectory" switch indicates that all files in subordinate subdirectories should be restored along with those in the specified directory.

/P The "prompt" switch tells DOS to prompt you before restoring any files changed since the last backup or with a read-only status (see chapter 6).

NOTE: *Make sure you maintain version compatibility when backing up and restoring files. The DOS message Incorrect DOS version will result if you attempt to RESTORE files that were saved with a different DOS version of BACKUP.*

Wildcard characters (* and ?) can be used to restore several files with one execution of the RESTORE utility. Common applications for the RESTORE utility are displayed below.

To restore every file with a .PIX extension on the source disk in drive B to the active directory (\GRAPHICS) in drive C.

```
C>cd \graphics ↵

C>restore b: c:*.pix ↵

Insert backup diskette 01 in drive B:
Strike any key when ready

*** Files were backed up 12/15/1988 ***

*** Restoring files from drive B: ***
Diskette: 01
\GRAPHICS\TITLEPG.PIX
\GRAPHICS\COVER.PIX

C>
```

To prompt user before restoring files from drive B to drive C.

```
C>restore b: c:*.* /p ↵

Insert backup diskette 01 in drive B:
Strike any key when ready

*** Files were backed up 10/01/1989 ***

*** Restoring files from drive B: ***
Diskette: 01
\ANNUAL89.RPT

Warning! File ANNUAL89.RPT
was changed after it was backed up
Replace the file (Y/N)?_
```

Response of Y or y allows DOS to replace new version with older file.

CHAPTER 5: HARD DISK MANAGEMENT

```
C>restore a: c:\WORDPROC\budget89.wks ↵

Insert backup diskette 01 in drive A:
Strike any key when ready

*** Files were backed up 01/06/1989 ***

*** Restoring files from drive A: ***
Diskette: 01
\WORDPROC\BUDGET89.WKS
```

To restore the file BUDGET89.WKS on the source disk in drive A to the target disk's \WORDPROC subdirectory.

```
B>restore a: c:\*.* /s ↵

Insert backup diskette 01 in drive A:
Strike any key when ready

*** Files were backed up 11/25/1988 ***

*** Restoring files from drive A: ***
Diskette: 01
\COMMAND.COM
\ANSI.SYS
   .   .
   .   .

Insert backup diskette 02 in drive A:
Strike any key when ready

*** Restoring files from drive A: ***
Diskette: 02
\WORDPROC\LETTERS\DK0121.LET
   .      .     .
   .      .     .
```

Restoring continues until every subdirectory is restored.

To restore all the files in every subdirectory on the source disk(s) in drive A to the target disk in drive C.

DOS MESSAGES

RESTORE

Invalid argument
> The argument, usually a switch, in your instruction line is not acceptable.

Invalid parameter(s)
> One of your switches is unacceptable.

File creation error
> This message can occur when there is not enough space for the file. Delete unnecessary files and try to RESTORE the file again.
>
> This error could also occur when attempting to RESTORE a read-only file. Use the ATTRIB utility discussed in Chapter 6 to turn the read-only attribute off and attempt to RESTORE the file again.

Restore file sequence in error
> The backup disks are in the wrong order, thus making the restore sequence wrong. Be careful about numbering the disks during backup. It also helps to store backup disks in the proper sequence.

EXPLORING DOS

11. What DOS command would restore the FORMAT program on the backup disk in drive A to its original form on drive C?

PROBLEM SOLVING WITH DOS

An important task for hard disk users is highlighted in this section: subdirectory preparation for software installation.

You are ready to add a full accounting package to your hard disk software library. Since the process of software selection involved the use of a demo package, some structuring of the hard disk has already taken place. The following diagram shows the current subdirectory structure.

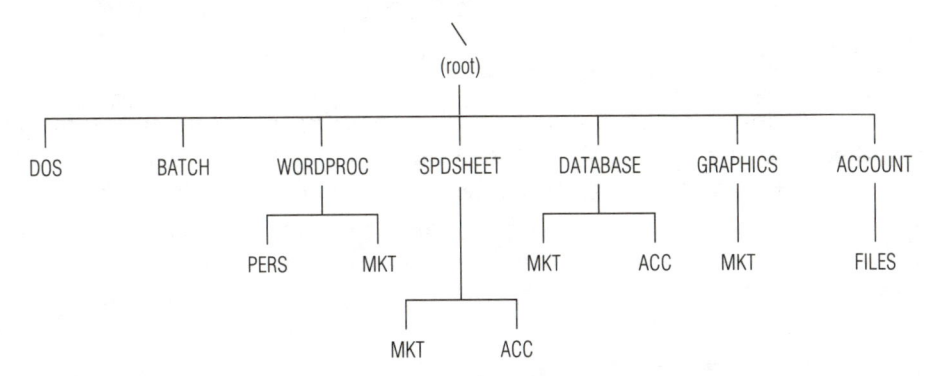

```
                              \
                           (root)
    ┌──────┬───────┬─────────┼─────────┬─────────┬─────────┐
   DOS   BATCH  WORDPROC  SPDSHEET  DATABASE  GRAPHICS  ACCOUNT
                  ┌─┴─┐      │       ┌─┴─┐       │         │
                 PERS MKT    │      MKT ACC     MKT      FILES
                          ┌──┴──┐
                         MKT   ACC
```

The demo accounting package currently installed needs to be removed and the complete package installed. Software needs to be loaded into the \ACCOUNT subdirectory. Only files associated with the accounting package should be in the \ACCOUNT subdirectory. This software is designed to work with the following subdirectories, which are expected to be subordinate to the \ACCOUNT directory.

General Ledger	**GLD**
Payroll	**PRL**
Accounts Receivable	**ARC**
Accounts Payable	**APL**
Job Costing	**JCT**
Transactions	**TRA**
Clients	**CLT**
Employees	**EMP**
Vendors	**VND**

PROBLEM 1

Design a hierarchy of subdirectories for the new accounting system.

Answer:

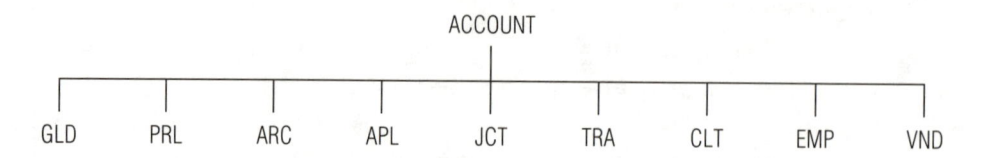

```
                          ACCOUNT
   ┌─────┬─────┬─────┬─────┼─────┬─────┬─────┐
  GLD   PRL   ARC   APL   JCT   TRA   CLT   EMP   VND
```

PROBLEM 2

Prior to setting up the new software, the existing structure needs to be modified. The FILES subdirectory subordinate to the ACCOUNT subdirectory should be removed and the current demo software in the ACCOUNT subdirectory deleted. List the exact steps involved in completing these tasks. Assume you are in the root directory.

Answer:

```
C>prompt $p$g ↵
C:\>cd c:\account\files ↵
C:\ACCOUNT\FILES>dir *.* ↵

Volume in drive C: is HARD DISK
Directory of C:\ACCOUNT\FILES

M0034256 GLD      5422    8-20-88    10:24a
M0034256 TRA     10022    8-20-88    10:32a
M0034256 RPT      2971    8-30-88     2:00p
   .       .        .        .          .
   .       .        .        .          .

    9 File(s)    13043789 bytes free

C:\ACCOUNT\FILES>del *.* ↵     Assuming what DIR displayed was acceptable.
```

CHAPTER 5: HARD DISK MANAGEMENT

```
C:\ACCOUNT\FILES>cd c:\account ↵
C:\ACCOUNT>rd files ↵
C:\ACCOUNT>dir *.* ↵


Volume in drive C: is HARD DISK
Directory of C:\ACCOUNT

ACC      EXE      78285    7-23-87    12:00p
GLD      OVL       6022    7-23-87    12:00p
GLD      RPT      13876    7-23-87    12:00p
 .        .         .        .          .
 .        .         .        .          .

15 File(s)     13121769 bytes free

C:\ACCOUNT>del *.* ↵          Assuming what DIR displayed was acceptable.
```

PROBLEM 3

Create the desired subdirectory structure that the accounting software expects to find in the ACCOUNT subdirectory.

Answer:

```
C:\ACCOUNT>md gld ↵
C:\ACCOUNT>md prl ↵
C:\ACCOUNT>md arc ↵
C:\ACCOUNT>md apl ↵
C:\ACCOUNT>md jct ↵
C:\ACCOUNT>md tra ↵
C:\ACCOUNT>md clt ↵
C:\ACCOUNT>md emp ↵
C:\ACCOUNT>md vnd ↵
```

```
C:\ACCOUNT>dir ↵         Check that all subdirectories are present.

Volume in drive C: is HARD DISK
Directory of C:\ACCOUNT

.            <DIR>     4-16-88    2:00p
..           <DIR>     4-16-88    2:00p
GLD          <DIR>     9-18-88    9:35a
PRL          <DIR>     9-18-88    9:35a
ARC          <DIR>     9-18-88    9:36a
APL          <DIR>     9-18-88    9:36a
JCT          <DIR>     9-18-88    9:36a
TRA          <DIR>     9-18-88    9:36a
CLT          <DIR>     9-18-88    9:36a
EMP          <DIR>     9-18-88    9:36a
VND          <DIR>     9-18-88    9:36a

   11 File(s)    13654884 bytes free
```

PROBLEM 4

With the subdirectory structure now set up for the accounting package, you should proceed to copy the files from the nine master disks into the ACCOUNT subdirectory. Place a write protect tab on each of the master disks before you start. If you are currently in drive C's root directory, what command would you employ if the source drive is drive A?

Answer:

```
C:\>copy a:*.* c:\account /v ↵
```

PROBLEM 5

What steps would you take to backup the nine master diskettes that contain the accounting package software?

Answer: Be sure you have enough disks to complete the backup of the master disks. Label each backup disk to coordinate with the master disks. Proceed to backup each master with the DISKCOPY utility.

Another approach would be to use the BACKUP utility to copy the accounting package from the ACCOUNT subdirectory to the floppy disks. If you use BACKUP, remember the new disks must be formatted first or you must include the /F switch in the BACKUP instruction line. This backup procedure provides a backup of the installed version of the software, which saves time if you have to reinstall the software due to a disk crash.

PROBLEM 6

When you try to backup the first master disk using DISKCOPY, the following DOS message appears on the screen:

```
C:\ACCOUNT>diskcopy a: a: ↵
Bad command or file not found
```

What does this message indicate, and how would you avoid this problem?

Answer: DISKCOPY is a utility program and the computer needs access to the DOS disk or DOS subdirectory on the hard disk.

Two solutions are possible:

1. *Set the search path to include the DOS subdirectory with PATH=C:\;C:\DOS*

2. *Include the path in the command line as illustrated below:*

```
C:\ACCOUNT>c:\dos\diskcopy a: a: ↵
```

PROBLEM 7

After using the accounting software for a week, it is time to backup the data files. Assume you are in the root directory and wish to backup to a floppy disk in drive A. How would you proceed to backup files in the ACCOUNT subdirectory and all subordinate subdirectories?

Answer: `C:\>backup c:\account a: /s /m` ↵

This command uses the subdirectory switch (/S) to backup files in the ACCOUNT directory and all its subdirectories. There are potentially two drawbacks to this approach. If you did not originally use the BACKUP utility to copy the accounting package from ACCOUNT, the program files are copied again along with the data files. Since the Modify switch (/M) is used, this problem only exists the first time the command line is employed. Subsequent use of this instruction line will only backup recently modified data files because program files are usually not updated.

ANSWERS TO EXPLORING DOS QUESTIONS

1. Yes, a newly formatted diskette's directory will include the \DOS and \WORKAREA listings and report there are 2 file(s) present.

2. Two directory references (. and ..) are included in the file list.

3. Approximately 1024 bytes (characters)

4. `PROMPT (yourlastname) $g`

5. No Path

6. `path=\DOS;WORKAREA`

7. `APPEND=\HOMEWORK`

8. Enter `APPEND` and press Enter key

9. Approximately 128 bytes

10. No, the creation time and date are the same for the backup and original.

11. `RESTORE a: c:FORMAT.???` (assuming backup is in drive A and original is in drive C).

6 Backup and Recovery

IN THIS CHAPTER:

ATTRIB
CHKDSK
COPY NUL
DISKCOPY
DISKCOMP
RECOVER
REPLACE

Storage media are always vulnerable. It is a lesson everyone learns the hard way. Even with the best care, disks will wear out. Hard disks have bearings that go bad, while floppy disks and tapes often fail due to wear caused by contact between the recording surface and the drive's read/write head. This chapter will show you how to identify bad disks, how to locate and recover lost data, and several procedures for creating backup copies of valuable files.

IDENTIFYING BAD DISKS WITH CHKDSK

Since disk failure is inevitable, the DOS CHKDSK utility provides microcomputer users with the means of identifying disks with **bad sectors** (damaged areas on a disk's recording surface) or lost data. The basic syntax used by CHKDSK is as follows:

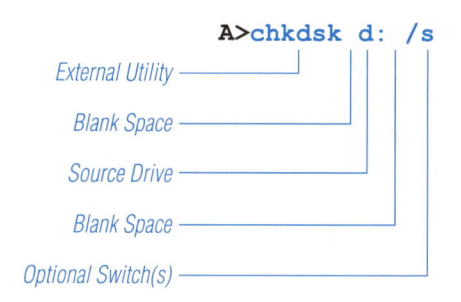

```
A>chkdsk d: /s
```

- External Utility
- Blank Space
- Source Drive
- Blank Space
- Optional Switch(s)

Running the CHKDSK utility results in a disk status report similar to the following example. The occurrence of bad sectors or lost data is reported if found. Notice that the status report also displays information related to the computer's current memory status. In this example the computer has 655,360 bytes (characters) of storage in main memory with 577,408 bytes still available for use.

Sample report displayed by using the CHKDSK utility.

```
Volume WORK DISK    created Aug 29, 1988 3:41p

362496 bytes total disk space
 38912 bytes in 2 hidden files
 35840 bytes in 20 user files
  2048 bytes in bad sectors
285692 bytes available on disk


655360 bytes total memory
577408 bytes free
```

Bad Sectors

While it is not unusual for hard disks to come from the factory with bad sectors (these sectors are identified and taken out of service by DOS when the hard disk is formatted), the random appearance of bad sectors on any disk is a sure sign of trouble. A bad sector can make the disk directory, file allocation table (FAT), data, or programs inaccessible. The loss of the directory or FAT is especially disastrous since they identify the contents and storage location of every data file and program stored on disk.

Fragmented Files

The CHKDSK utility also identifies badly *fragmented files* and lost data clusters. Files are fragmented (broken into several parts and stored in physically separate locations) when there is not enough sequential disk space to store them. Large files stored on heavily used disks are often fragmented. Fragmenting files is a standard DOS activity and normally should not concern the user. However, badly fragmented files (many non-contiguous segments) can slow disk reading and writing activities. CHKDSK can report the number of non-contiguous segments associated with a given file. For example, you would enter the following if the file TECBROC was suspected of being badly fragmented:

```
A>chkdsk b:tecbroc
```

If the file is fragmented, the computer will display, after the status report, a message similar to the one listed below:

> **B:\TECBROC**
> **Contains 23 non-contiguous blocks.**

In this case TECBROC has been fragmented into twenty-three segments. The More on the COPY Command section found later in this chapter describes how to unite badly fragmented files.

Lost Clusters

Lost clusters result from unexpected interruptions of file processing activities. A power failure when working with large data files or the accidental opening of a floppy disk drive door while writing to disk can interrupt standard disk output operations. As a result, DOS does not properly identify the location of some file segments in the FAT. These misplaced file segments become *lost clusters*.

You should periodically run CHKDSK on each disk to ensure the integrity of the disk and files. Furthermore, many DOS users automatically run CHKDSK as a part of booting procedures (see Chapter 7 discussion of AUTOEXEC.BAT files).

NOTE: *When executing the CHKDSK utility, DOS assumes the disk is already in the drive and does not wait for the user to insert the disk as it does with the FORMAT utility.*

CHKDSK utilizes two switches:

/F When the "fix" switch is specified, DOS recovers lost clusters and assigns each a name starting with FILE0000.CHK. Therefore, if four lost clusters are found on a disk, DOS identifies them as FILE0000.CHK, FILE0001.CHK, FILE0002.CHK, FILE0003.CHK. The contents of these files can be examined with TYPE command (Chapter 4: File Output to the Screen or Printer) or word processing software and renamed, if desired.

/V The "volume" switch is primarily used with hard disks. This switch displays all the files, including hidden files, on disk and their associated subdirectories (see Chapter 5: Hard Disk Management).

The following screen displays represent common applications of the CHKDSK utility.

To display a disk status report for a disk in the default drive A.

```
A>chkdsk

Volume DTP           created Aug 9, 1988 2:25p

362496 bytes total disk space
  2892 bytes in 1 hidden files
 35840 bytes in 20 user files
326656 bytes available on disk

655360 bytes total memory
577408 bytes free
```

To locate and fix lost clusters of data on the disk in drive C.

```
A>chkdsk c: /f

8 lost clusters found in 2 chains
Convert lost chains to files (Y/N)?y
```
*Responding with a **Y** or **y** recovers lost clusters.*

```
31977472 bytes total disk space
   38912 bytes in 2 hidden files
   71680 bytes in 26 directories
17072128 bytes in 1170 user files
    4096 bytes in 1 recovered files
14743552 bytes available on disk

  655360 bytes total memory
  577408 bytes free
```

```
C>chkdsk /v ↵

Directory C:\
C:\IBMBIO.COM
C:\IBMDOS.COM
C:\COMMAND.COM
Directory C:\DOS
C:\DOS\CHKDSK.COM
C:\DOS\BACKUP.COM
C:\DOS\RESTORE.COM
C:\DOS\DISKCOPY.COM
C:\DOS\RECOVER.COM
   .    .    .
   .    .    .
   .    .    .
Directory C:\WS
C:\WS\WSU.COM
C:\WS\WSOVLY1.OVR
   .    .    .
   .    .    .
   .    .    .


31977472 bytes total disk space
   38912 bytes in 2 hidden files
   71680 bytes in 26 directories
17039360 bytes in 1169 user files
   51200 bytes in bad sectors
14776320 bytes available on disk

  655360 bytes total memory
  577408 bytes free
```

To display a disk status report and file organization by subdirectories on the default hard disk drive C.

To look for non-contiguous files on disk in drive B.

```
A>chkdsk b:*.* ↵

Volume BROCHURE     created Feb 3, 1988 6:59p

362496 bytes total disk space
 37888 bytes in 3 hidden files
322560 bytes in 76 user files
  2048 bytes available on disk

655360 bytes total memory
577408 bytes free

A:\TECBROC
Contains 23 non-contiguous blocks.
A:\ROBOT.SLD
Contains 2 non-contiguous blocks.
A:\WIDGET.GEM
Contains 2 non-contiguous blocks.
```

DOS MESSAGES

CHKDSK

Errors found, F parameter not specified
Corrections will not be written to disk

8 lost cluster(s) found in 2 chains
Convert lost chains to files (Y/N)?y ↵

730112 bytes total disk space
      NOTE: *720K 3.5" drive.*
    0 bytes in 1 user files

```
        4096 bytes would be in
           1 recovered files
      726016 bytes available on disk
```

The CHKDSK utility has discovered information on the disk that isn't allocated properly in the disk's File Allocation Table (FAT). The message **Corrections will not be written to disk** indicates CHKDSK was executed without the /F switch (parameter); therefore, the user is being informed that no corrections will be made.

By answering yes to the "convert lost chains" prompt, however, you get a report of what action would occur from the fix switch. It is recommended that you reexecute the CHKDSK utility with the /F switch to fix the file and free disk space that is allocated but not in use. The resulting status report looks like this:

```
A>chkdsk b: /f ↵

      730112 bytes total disk space
           0 bytes in 1 user files
        4096 bytes in 1 recovered files
      726016 bytes available on disk
```

Now you can examine FILE0000.CHK and use any recoverable portions of the file.

```
B:\REPORT06.DOC
    Contains 4 non-contiguous blocks
```

This DOS message simply indicates that the file is stored on disk as fragmented segments. There is no indication that there is anything wrong with the file; thus, no action on your part is immediately indicated. Should you have a large number of fragmented files on the disk it may be worthwhile to use COPY *.* to copy the disk files to a newly formatted disk. By copying the files to a blank disk, they will be in contiguous blocks, which enhances disk response time.

> ### EXPLORING DOS
>
> *Run CHKDSK on your DOS disk.*
>
> **1. How many hidden files are there?**
>
> **2. How many user files are there?**
>
> **3. How many bytes are still available on disk?**
>
> **4. How many bytes are still available in memory?**

DISKCOPY

Knowing that storage media are vulnerable to damage, loss, and theft leads the experienced user to one conclusion: backup important files on a second and even a third disk. Individual files can easily be backed up using the COPY command. Copying the contents of one disk to another is often accomplished with the COPY command using wild cards (*.*). However, these procedures require a formatted disk and do not copy the hidden system files discussed in Chapter 7.

The DISKCOPY utility was specifically written to backup the contents of one diskette to a new, unformatted diskette. This utility also copies any hidden files present on the disk. Previously formatted diskettes can also be used as a target disk. Using formatted disks decreases the time it takes to complete the disk copy.

NOTE: *When a formatted disk is used as the target disk, the contents will be erased and replaced with incoming data from the source disk.*

The general format for the external DISKCOPY utility is as follows:

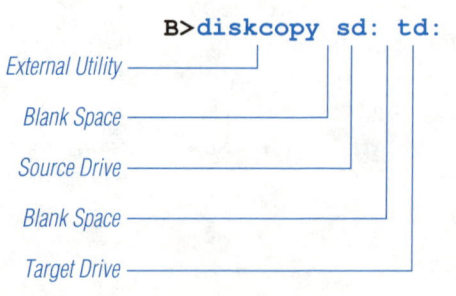

```
B>diskcopy sd: td:
```

- External Utility
- Blank Space
- Source Drive
- Blank Space
- Target Drive

CHAPTER 6: BACKUP AND RECOVERY

If an unformatted disk is found in the target disk drive, DOS will format the target disk before copying the contents from the source disk. An error message will result if you try to use DISKCOPY with a hard disk or the target disk has a write protect tab in place. In addition, the source drive and target drive must contain identical media. For example, both disks would have to be 3-1/2 inch double-sided, double-density diskettes. Do not copy the contents of a high-density diskette to a double-density diskette or vice versa. The following screens demonstrate some of the common uses of DISKCOPY.

```
C>diskcopy a: b: ↵

Insert SOURCE Diskette in Drive A:

Insert TARGET Diskette in Drive B:

Press any key when ready...

Copying 40 tracks
9 Sectors/Track, 2 Side(s)

Formatting While Copying

Copy another diskette (Y/N)?_
```

To copy the contents of the disk in drive A to an unformatted disk in drive B.

```
C>diskcopy b: a: ↵

Insert SOURCE Diskette in Drive B:

Insert TARGET Diskette in Drive A:

Press any key when ready...

Copying 40 tracks
9 Sectors/Track, 2 Side(s)

Copy another diskette (Y/N)?_
```

To copy the contents of disk in drive B to a formatted disk in drive A.

To use DISKCOPY with a single floppy disk drive system.

```
A>diskcopy ↵

Insert SOURCE Diskette in Drive A:
Press any key when ready...


Copying 40 tracks
9 Sectors/Track, 2 Side(s)


Insert TARGET Diskette in Drive A:
Press any key when ready...


Copy another diskette (Y/N)?_
```

D O S   M E S S A G E S

DISKCOPY

Target disk is write protected
The disk you are using as the target disk has a write-protect tab on it. You can simply remove the tab; however, the tag's presence would indicate that the data was important at one time. Since DISKCOPY erases the current contents of the target disk, use DIR /P to check the contents of the disk before you remove the tab and proceed with the diskcopy.

Target disk may be unusable
The disk you are using as a target disk is bad. Before discarding the disk you could attempt to format it with the FORMAT utility.

Bad command or missing filename
You misspelled DISKCOPY or have failed to identify the proper location of the external DISKCOPY utility program. Use DIR command to locate utility program and try again.

Invalid drive specification.
Specified drive does not exist,
or is non-removable.
> *You are trying to DISKCOPY from a hard disk or forgot to identify either the source or target disk drive. Try again using drive designations for floppy disk drives.*

Invalid parameter
Do not specify filename(s)
> *Only floppy disk drive designations are allowed in the instruction line. Enter the instruction again without using a filename.*

EXPLORING DOS

5. How would you backup a DOS disk that has hidden files?

COMPARING DISKS

Many DOS users like to double-check that the DISKCOPY utility made a perfect copy of the original disk. The external DISKCOMP (disk compare) utility program performs this service. The standard format for DISKCOMP follows:

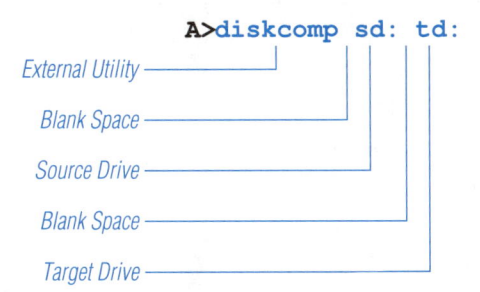

```
A>diskcomp sd: td:
```
- External Utility
- Blank Space
- Source Drive
- Blank Space
- Target Drive

The DISKCOMP utility program only works with floppy disks. Furthermore, you must compare identical media. For example, both disks would have to be

5-1/4 inch double-sided, double-density floppy disks. Do not try to compare a high-density disk with a double-density disk.

When executing this instruction, DOS make a sector by sector comparison of both disks. An error message will result if the comparison reveals any differences between the disk data. Like DISKCOPY, this utility program will work with single floppy disk systems. When using DISKCOMP on a single floppy disk system, DOS will prompt users to swap disks. Common applications for DISKCOMP are demonstrated in the following screen displays.

To compare the diskette in drive A with one in drive B.

```
A>diskcomp a: b: ↵

Insert FIRST  diskette in drive A:
Insert SECOND diskette in drive B:
Press any key when ready...

Comparing 80 cylinders
9 sectors per track, 2 side(s)

Compare OK

Compare another diskette (Y/N)?_
```
                          Enter N to return to DOS prompt.

To compare floppy disks on a single disk drive system.

```
A>diskcomp ↵

Insert FIRST  diskette in drive A:
Press any key when ready...

Comparing 40 cylinders
9 sectors per track, 2 side(s)
```

```
Insert SECOND diskette in drive B:
Press any key when ready...


Compare OK


Compare another diskette (Y/N)?_
```

D O S   M E S S A G E S

DISKCOMP

Compare error on cylinder X, side X

The data on the target disk do not match the original. If the target disk is a recent DISKCOPY of the source disk, a problem could exist. Make a new backup with DISKCOPY. Files copied to a target disk with the COPY command WILL NOT result in an identical compare; however, this does not necessarily indicate a problem with either disk.

Invalid parameter
Do not specify filename(s)

Only floppy disk drive designations are allowed in the instruction line. Enter the instruction again without using a filename.

Bad command or missing filename

You misspelled DISKCOMP or have failed to identify the proper location of the external DISKCOMP utility program. Use DIR command to locate the DISKCOMP utility program and try again.

Invalid drive specification.
Specified drive does not exist,
or is non-removable.

You are trying to DISKCOMP from a hard disk or forgot to identify either the source or target disk drive. Try again using drive designations for floppy disk drives.

> # EXPLORING DOS
>
> **6.** How would you check that the DISKCOPY you made in Exploring DOS 5 was executed without errors?

REPLACING OLD BACKUPS WITH NEW

While the COPY command and DISKCOPY utility allow you to create backup copies of important data and programs, the DOS REPLACE utility is useful when these files need updating. Newer versions of DOS (from 3.2 and on) include the REPLACE utility. It allows you to update only those backup files that predate their counterparts on the designated source disk.

The standard syntax for the REPLACE command looks like this:

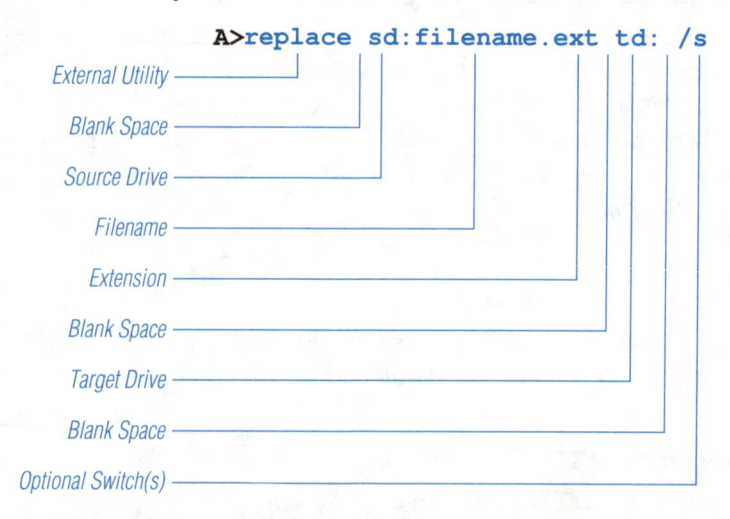

```
A>replace sd:filename.ext td: /s
```

- External Utility
- Blank Space
- Source Drive
- Filename
- Extension
- Blank Space
- Target Drive
- Blank Space
- Optional Switch(s)

The following switches make REPLACE a versatile DOS utility:

/A The "add" switch inserts, instead of replaces, new files not on the target disk that are found on the source disk. Files existing on both the target and source disk are not replaced. This switch cannot be used with the /D or /S switches.

/D The "dated" switch replaces files on the target disk only when a newer version is found on the source disk. You cannot use this switch along with the /A switch. This switch is not on PC-DOS versions through 3.3. PC-DOS 4.0 uses a /U "update" switch, which works in the same way.

/P The "prompt" switch displays the message Replace FILENAME.EXT? (Y/N) which allows you to selectively replace files on the target disk.

/R The "read-only" switch replaces read-only files (see the next section on Setting File Attributes for more details) and unprotected files. If this switch is not used, a DOS error message is displayed and the replace process is stopped when DOS attempts to replace a read-only file.

/S The "subdirectory" switch indicates that you want DOS to replace files on all relevant subdirectories found on the target disk. When this switch is used, every file on the target disk with a matching file on the source disk will be replaced, no matter where it is located. You cannot use this switch along with the /A switch.

/W The "wait" switch forces DOS to wait for you to press any key on the keyboard before it begins replacing files. This switch is particularly useful to people with single disk systems who need to swap disks before the REPLACE process begins. If this switch is not used, the replacing begins as soon as the DOS utility name and optional switches are entered.

NOTE: *REPLACE does not work with hidden system files (see Chapter 7 for more details).*

The following screen displays show some of the common applications for REPLACE and its associated switches.

```
C>replace a:*.dat b: ↵

 Replacing B:\QUIZ1.DAT

 Replacing B:\QUIZ2.DAT

 Replacing B:\QUIZ3.DAT

 Replacing B:\FINAL.DAT

 Access denied  'B:\FINAL.DAT'

 3 File(s) replaced
```

The fifth file never gets replaced because the fourth file is read-only, and replacing is aborted.

To replace every file that has a .DAT extension in drive B with the current version from the disk in drive A. The fourth of the five files is a read-only file.

To replace every file that has a .DAT extension in drive B with current version from drive A, using Read-only switch (/R). The fourth of five files is a read-only file:

```
C>replace a:*.dat b: /r ↵

 Replacing B:\QUIZ1.DAT

 Replacing B:\QUIZ2.DAT

 Replacing B:\QUIZ3.DAT

 Replacing B:\FINAL.DAT

 Replacing B:\QUIZ4.DAT

5 File(s) replaced
```

To add files to the target disk in drive B that exist on the source disk in drive A but not on the target disk, with a wait for user's key press before beginning.

```
C>replace a:*.*  b: /a /w ↵

Press any key to begin adding file(s)

Adding B:\FILE1.DAT
Adding B:\FILE2.DAT
Adding B:\FILE3.DAT
Adding B:\FILE4.DAT
Adding B:\FILE5.DAT
Adding B:\FILE6.DAT
Adding B:\FILE7.DAT
Adding B:\FILE8.DAT

8 File(s) added
```

```
C>replace b:test?.dat a: /d /p ↵

Replace A:\TEST1.DAT? (Y/N)y ↵           User enters y.

Replacing B:\TEST1.DAT
      .     .     .
      .     .     .
      .     .     .
Replacing B:\TEST3.DAT

3 File(s) added
```

To ask if user wants to replace files on target disk in drive A with the same files from the source disk in drive B having newer creation dates.

DOS MESSAGES

REPLACE

No files found 'A:\filename.ext'
No files added

> This message is generated when the optional /A switch is used with the REPLACE utility. In this case, no new files were found on the source disk to add to the target disk. The most common cause of this message is failure to use valid filenames or absence of the designated files on the source disk. The key to solving this problem is the first line of the DOS message. It lists the filename upon which adding is based. Use this information to confirm that the files you wish to add are present on the proper disk.

Access denied

> DOS displays this message and aborts execution when it tries to replace a read-only file. Use the F3 function key to recall the instruction line and add /R. This switch tells DOS you want to replace all the identified files, including those marked read-only.

> **No files found 'A:\filename.ext'**
> **No files replaced**
>
> *The most common cause of this message is failure to use valid filenames or absence of the designated files on the source disk. The key to solving this problem is the first line of the DOS message. It lists the file that DOS thinks you want to replace. Use this information to confirm that the files you wish to replace are present on both the target and source disks.*
>
> **Parameters not compatible**
> **No files replaced**
>
> *You have used two switches with the replace utility that are not compatible with one another. For example, you cannot use the /A and /D switches together. The basis for switch incompatibility is in any attempt to combine FILE ADD and FILE REPLACE features in the same command.*

EXPLORING DOS

7. How would you use the REPLACE utility to backup the USER.DOC file on your work disk?

SETTING FILE ATTRIBUTES

The DOS attribute utility (ATTRIB) gives you the option of modifying some of the attributes of a disk file. The external ATTRIB utility program enables you to set file archive bits and the read-only bit used by the REPLACE utility and other DOS instructions. When the read-only bit is turned on (+r), associated files can be used and copied but not overwritten or erased. With the archive bit on (+a), DOS assumes that the files have not been backed up or have been modified since the last backup.

The archive bit (a) is used by DOS at the time a file is initially created (written) or updated (modified). The REPLACE utility (along with BACKUP and RESTORE discussed in Chapter 5) uses the archive bit to determine which files need to be backed up or restored. Knowledge of the ATTRIB utility and the use of the archive bit are useful in developing customized backup routines for hard disk computers (see Appendix E: Practical Batch Files). The read-only bit (r) can protect files from inadvertent erasure. For example, setting the read-only bit on your DOS files or form letters is a good idea. The standard syntax for the ATTRIB utility is listed below:

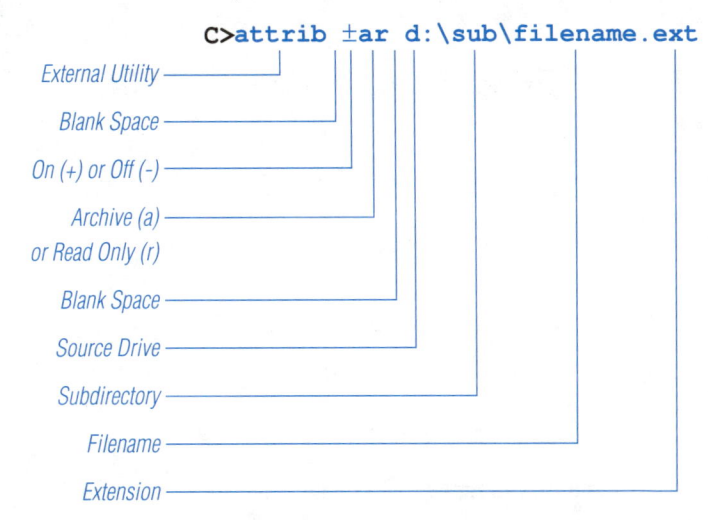

```
C>attrib ±ar d:\sub\filename.ext
```

- External Utility
- Blank Space
- On (+) or Off (-)
- Archive (a) or Read Only (r)
- Blank Space
- Source Drive
- Subdirectory
- Filename
- Extension

NOTE: *If the ATTRIB utility is executed without setting either the archive or read-only attributes, DOS will report the status of the attributes of the indicated file(s).*

The ATTRIB utility uses the plus sign (+) to indicate that the archive bit (+a) or the read-only bit (+r) should be turned on. The minus sign (–) sets the associated bit to off. Once the read-only bit is set on, it can only be changed by resetting it with the attribute utility. Copying a file will set the bit on (+a) while backing up the file will turn it off (–a). The following screen displays demonstrate common applications of the ATTRIB utility.

```
C>attrib +r c:\dos\*.* ↵
C>
```

To protect the files in the \DOS subdirectory by setting them to read-only.

To display a status report of current attribute setting for files in the \DOS subdirectory.

```
C>attrib c:\dos\*.*  ↵

   R     C:\DOS\COMMAND.COM
   R         .
   R         .
   R         .
```

To display current attribute setting for files in \INVOICE\FILES subdirectory. The first 2 files are read-only and the last two files have the archive bit on.

```
C>attrib c:\invoice\files\*.*  ↵

         R    C:\INVOICE\FILES\FORM0001.STY
         R    C:\INVOICE\FILES\FORM0002.STY
              C:\INVOICE\FILES\654A0430.INV
              C:\INVOICE\FILES\716A0513.INV
         A    C:\INVOICE\FILES\654A0921.INV
         A    C:\INVOICE\FILES\716A1030.INV
```

D O S   M E S S A G E S

ATTRIB

Bad command or file name

You misspelled ATTRIB, you did not specify where to find the ATTRIB utility, or you are using a DOS version prior to DOS 3.0.

File not found
> *You misspelled the filename or did not specify the correct subdirectory location for the file. Use the DIR command to locate the file and verify the filename's correct spelling.*

Invalid number of parameters
> *You tried to use more than one attribute in the same command line. Set either the read-only attribute or archive attribute.*

Syntax error
> *You have entered the command line incorrectly. Make sure you leave the proper spacing between ATTRIB, the attribute setting, and filename(s).*

EXPLORING DOS

8. How would you set the files on your DOS disk in drive A to read-only?

RECOVERING LOST FILES

Unfortunately, almost everyone eventually is forced to face the problem of recovering important data from a bad disk. When this happens, the RECOVER utility (and special applications of the COPY command outlined in the next section) can help you minimize and sometimes recover from the problem.

The RECOVER utility can help in two ways. First, it can be used to recover a single file with bad sectors. In this case, as much of the file as possible is saved. Sections of data associated with the bad sector(s) will still be missing and some editing of the file is necessary to remove unwanted characters and data that have become embedded in the file as part of the recovery process.

The second application for RECOVER concerns bad sectors in the disk directory or file allocation table (FAT). These situations are more serious since they render the disk unreadable. In this case DOS tries to recover every file, creates a new disk directory and FAT, gives every file a new name starting with FILE0001.REC, and places the recovered files (even those originating in subdirectories) in the \ (root) directory. Two general forms of the RECOVER utility are used depending on whether you are recovering a single file or the whole disk. Use the following syntax to recover a single file:

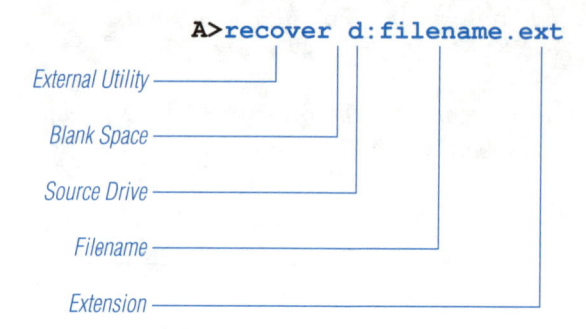

```
A>recover d:filename.ext
```

- External Utility
- Blank Space
- Source Drive
- Filename
- Extension

NOTE: *RECOVER does not recognize wild cards characters and only recovers one file at a time when a filename is specified in the command line.*

The format below is used in an attempt to recover the contents of every file on the designated disk:

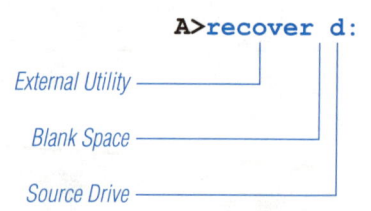

```
A>recover d:
```

- External Utility
- Blank Space
- Source Drive

Recovering an entire disk not only renames every data and program file on the disk, it also renames all the subdirectories. Therefore, only use this option as a last resort when the disk directory or file allocation table (FAT) is unusable. This application of the RECOVER utility creates a new disk directory, and every file (good or bad) is renamed and repositioned in the FAT. Since the recovery process can potentially find and add miscellaneous data from deleted files, it is important that users examine the content of every renamed file.

The two primary applications for RECOVER are demonstrated in the following screen displays.

```
C>recover b:tv.dat ↵

Press any key to begin recovery of the
file(s) on drive B:

384 of 512 bytes recovered
```

To recover a single file from a disk in drive B.

```
C>recover a: ↵

Press any key to begin recovery of the
file(s) on drive A:

12 file(s) recovered

C>dir a: ↵

 Volume in drive A has no label
 Directory of  A:\

FILE0001 REC      1536   8-14-88   10:56a
FILE0002 REC       512   8-14-88   10:56a
FILE0003 REC      1024   8-14-88   10:56a
FILE0004 REC       512   8-14-88   10:56a
FILE0005 REC       512   8-14-88   10:56a
FILE0006 REC       512   8-14-88   10:56a
FILE0007 REC       512   8-14-88   10:56a
FILE0008 REC       512   8-14-88   10:56a
FILE0009 REC       512   8-14-88   10:56a
FILE0010 REC       512   8-14-88   10:56a
FILE0011 REC       512   8-14-88   10:56a
FILE0012 REC       512   8-14-88   10:56a

       12 File(s)    187104 bytes free
```

To recover every file from the bad disk in drive A and display the disk directory after recovery is complete.

> ## D O S   M E S S A G E S
>
> ### RECOVER
>
> **Invalid drive or file name**
> *You have most likely failed to enter a drive designation with the utility or have misspelled the filename.*
>
> **File not found**
> *The filename you have included with the recover utility does not exist, is not on the indicated drive, or is misspelled. Use the DIR command to locate the file and verify the filename's correct spelling.*

> ## E X P L O R I N G   D O S
>
> 9. What happens when you use the RECOVER utility to recover USER.DOC, which you created in an earlier Exploring DOS?

MORE ON THE COPY COMMAND

Once again the COPY command, in one of its many permutations, can help DOS users. It can easily be used to consolidate fragmented files. Furthermore, those DOS users with versions of DOS that do not support the RECOVER utility can locate bad files and attempt to recover them using the COPY command.

Uniting Fragmented Files

If you discover a badly fragmented file there is no need for concern. DOS fragments a file when it cannot store the data in a contiguous set of sectors. DOS uses the file allocation table (FAT) to keep track of the location and proper order of the various segments. File fragmentation happens most often with large files and/or on full disks. This situation can become a nuisance, as disk read/write operations are slowed due to the need to jump from one segment to another when the computer performs input or output.

The solution to this problem is quite simple: Copy the files from the fragmented disk to a newly formatted disk using COPY *.*. By using the COPY command with an empty disk, DOS stores the files in sequential disk sectors, thereby eliminating the fragmentation problems. The old,fragmented copy can become the backup, while the new copy becomes the active version. DISKCOPY cannot be used since it makes an exact duplicate of the file on the second disk.

Locating Bad Files Using Copy

The CHKDSK utility will tell you there are bad sectors on a disk, but does not indicate which files contain the bad sectors. However, it is possible to use the COPY command to identify specific files with bad sectors. Look for the DOS message **Abort, Retry or Fail?** (older versions of DOS display Abort, Retry, Ignore?) when you instruct DOS to copy each file, one at a time. This message identifies files with bad sectors because DOS cannot COPY these damaged files.

When experienced DOS users take their best shot at identifying bad files, they use a special dummy device name (NUL) and the /B "binary read" switch. The /B switch forces DOS to read the file as if it were in binary code. As a result, data are not misinterpreted as an end-of-file mark, which tricks DOS into thinking it has finished reading the file. You can copy files to NUL with the following command line:

```
A>copy b:*.* NUL /b
```

All the files on the source disk in the B drive are copied to the dummy device, i.e., nowhere. The originals are left intact on drive B. In the process of reading the files from the source disk, the DOS message **Abort, Retry or Fail?** will appear when DOS cannot copy a file due to bad sectors (or other difficulties). Enter the F option (for fail) and continue copying all the files to the NUL device. In this way you can easily identify those files with problems.

Recovering Bad Files Using Copy

If you are using a version of DOS that does not support the RECOVER utility, COPYing files to a backup disk provides some opportunities for recovering data from disks with bad sectors. The DOS message **Abort, Retry or Fail?** is an invaluable option associated with the COPY command since it allows you to retry as many times as you like. Furthermore, using the Fail option can help you recover selected portions of the file not affected by the bad sectors. In this situation, DISKCOPY will not work because it will either duplicate bad data or abort the copy if it encounters physical damage to the disk.

If you suspect an important disk is going bad, immediately try to COPY its contents to a new, formatted disk. For example, the following command would COPY the contents of the source disk in drive A to the target disk in drive B:

```
C>copy  a:*.*  b:
```

One of two things will happen. In the best case, the source disk will copy without difficulty. As a result, you have a new backup copy of the disk just in case something does happen in the future. Running CHKDSK on the original disk might be wise at this point as well.

In the worst case, The DOS message **Abort, Retry or Fail?** will appear as DOS attempts to copy the files from the source disk. Depending on how important the files are, press R for Retry from two to 10 times. If the DOS message **Abort, Retry or Fail?** continues to appear without any ensuing disk activity, press F for Fail. In this way you might partially recover some of the file's content. If you must use the Fail option, be prepared to extensively edit the file since a variety of odd characters and data will probably appear in the file. Continue with this procedure, pressing Retry a few times and then Fail, until all the files have been copied.

To see if FILE1.DOC in drive B has bad sectors by copying it to NUL.

```
A>copy b:file1.doc nul /b ↵

B:FILE1.DOC
    1 file(s) copied
```
This file has no bad sectors, since it copied without problems.
```
A>copy b:file1.doc nul /b ↵

B:FILE1.DOC
Disk error reading drive B:
Abort, Retry, Fail?
```
This file has bad sectors, enter A to return to new DOS prompt.

PROBLEM SOLVING WITH DOS

Disk failures and attempted file recovery are the subjects of this section. The issue here is not one of learning what to do IF disaster strikes but what to do WHEN it happens. At some time one of these problems, or a similar experience, will happen to you. So be prepared! The best three pieces of advice that can be given are: BACKUP, BACKUP, and BACKUP.

PROBLEM 1

For the last hour you have been word processing a very important report. As you are saving the file (REPORT01.DOC) to a disk there is an interruption in the power and your computer blanks out. It then reboots as the power comes back. When you list the directory of your data disk your worst fears are realized.

```
A>dir b: ↵

Volume in drive B is WORK DISK
Directory of B:\

REPORT01.DOC      0      12-18-88   7:20p

    1 File(s)     726016 bytes free
```

Since the file is listed in the directory, you try to display it with the TYPE command and get the following response:

```
A>type b:report01.doc ↵

A>
```

After this failure, is it worth the time in attempting to recover the apparently lost file?

Answer: YES! Recovery of a lost file, especially an important one, is always worth the effort. Since this is the only file on the disk you can easily identify from the final byte count that 4,096 bytes of disk space have been allocated to something, probably lost clusters. This number was obtained by using the CHKDSK utility and subtracting the byte count of the directory command from the total capacity of the disk, in this case 730112 - 726016 = 4096. This is a strong indication that there are some data in the REPORT01.DOC file even though the directory listing indicates 0.

You have two options for attempted recovery.

```
A>chkdsk b: /f
    or
A>recover b:report.doc
```

With the CHKDSK option one of two things will most likely take place. In the simplest case the utility will report:

```
Allocation error, size adjusted
```

After which, the file REPORT.DOC will show 4096 bytes. The other CHKDSK possibility is that the recovered file will be written to a new file called FILE0000.CHK. With the RECOVER option, the file FILE0001.REC will be created containing 4096 bytes. In both cases some of your hard work has been saved.

PROBLEM 2

In the process of making a backup of a disk with the DISKCOPY utility, you get a `Copy process ended` DOS message. Or worst yet, you get a `Read fault error` message. What should you do?

Answer: Since there is the distinct possibility that there still are valid data on your source disk, you should remove the disk from the drive and attach a write-protect tab. The write-protect tab will help prevent any mistakes on your part when trying to recover the files on this disk.

Once the write-protect tab is in place, your next step is to reinsert the disk in the drive and attempt the diskcopy again. The source disk may have been poorly seated in the drive, thus causing the error. If, however, the errors continue, your best bet is to attempt to copy the disk using the COPY *.* command. If you encounter an **Abort, Retry, Fail?** message, press the R key several times. If the message continues, press the F key to Fail. DOS will ignore the error and continue the copy process. Repeat this procedure as often as necessary until the copy process is completed.

If the copy command does not recover any files, then you would be best advised to use one of the commercially available file recovery utilities.

You may be asking at this point why the CHKDSK /F or RECOVER utilities have not been suggested. The reason is that both of these utilities attempt to write damaged files to new files **on the source disk** and the write-protect tab will have to come off. Should you make a mistake or if the process goes bad, you run the risk of losing data that might be recovered through other means.

The CHKDSK utility is much less of a risk in that it does not change the original files, but any writing to the damaged source disk at this point is a potential danger. Of course if you see your situation as "last ditch," then try CHKDSK /F first. If this is not successful go ahead and try RECOVER.

PROBLEM 3

As in Problem 2, you get a **Copy process ended** or **Read fault error** DOS message when backing up data using DISKCOPY. However, in this case COPY *.*, CHKDSK /F, and RECOVER all fail. What could you have done to avoid this problem?

Answer: The answer to this question really begins before the problem occurs. You need to make regular backups of your files on other disks that are stored in a secure location. When a sound backup procedure is maintained, problems such as these don't have nearly the degree of negative impact on productivity.

PROBLEM 4

You have updated a number of files and would like to update the backup files without doing a lengthy diskcopy. What is your best option?

Answer: If you are using DOS 3.2 or later versions, you can use the REPLACE utility to update the backup files.

PROBLEM 5

You have a dual floppy disk system. When using REPLACE the following DOS message appears on the screen:

```
A>replace a: b: ↵
Bad command or file name
```

Answer: REPLACE *is an external utility and you will need the DOS disk in drive A when executing this command. Use the Wait (/W) switch to give yourself time to replace the DOS disk with the appropriate source disk.*

PROBLEM 6

Taking the advice given in Problem 5, you put the DOS disk in drive A and use the Wait switch. Now this DOS message is displayed:

```
A>replace a: b: /w ↵
No files found 'A:\'
No files replaced
```

Answer: No file names were indicated in the command line executing the utility. You must use specific filenames or filenames that include wild card characters. One way or another you must indicate which files you wish replace by name. The REPLACE utility does use defaults in regard to filenames.

PROBLEM 7

Having learned a valuable lesson from Problems 5 and 6, you have a DOS disk in drive A and have included a specific filename in the command line. As a result, a new error message is now displayed on the screen:

```
A>replace report05.doc b: ↵

No file found A:\REPORT05.DOC

No files replaced
```

Answer: The file you wish to use as the source for the replacement is not on the disk in drive A, because this is the system disk. The problem then is that REPLACE did not give you the opportunity to change disks. This happened because you did not use the Wait (/W) switch.

SOLUTION

The proper use of the REPLACE utility that eliminates the error messages described in Problems 5, 6, and 7 is shown below:

```
A>replace a:report05.doc b: /w ↵

Press any key to begin replacing file(s)
```

ANSWERS TO EXPLORING DOS QUESTIONS

1. Either two or three.

2. There are approximately 20 to 75 user files on the DOS disk. The actual number will vary between versions of DOS.

3. Anywhere from zero to several thousand depending on your version of DOS and the type of disk on which it is stored.

4. Depends on the computer you are using.

5. Use DISKCOPY.

6. Use DISKCOMP.

7. Use REPLACE utility with /A switch.

8. **ATTRIB +r A:*.***

9. After entering RECOVER USER.DOC, DOS prompts you with the following message and then displays a new DOS prompt:

    ```
    Press any key to begin recovery of the
    file(s) on drive B:
    xxxx of xxxx bytes recovered
    ```

7 Customizing Your System

IN THIS CHAPTER:

BREAK
BUFFERS
COUNTRY
FCBS
FILES
DEVICE
DRIVPARM
LASTDRIVE
SHELL

Microcomputers enhance personal productivity in many ways. The wide variety of high-quality application software currently on the market is the foundation for this versatility. Adding dramatically to this power is the increasing number of hardware options available. As a result, knowledgeable microcomputer users can create personal configurations of hardware and software products that help them effectively accomplish desired tasks.

As you gravitate to easier-to-use and increasingly sophisticated software, new system programs will be working with DOS. For example, high-quality color displays and mice come with their own system programs. These ***device drivers*** identify the operating characteristics of the new I/O device, and they may require changes in system defaults that you set in DOS. In this chapter you will examine how to use DOS to customize your microcomputer system while enhancing system performance.

DEFINING HARDWARE/SOFTWARE RELATIONSHIPS

DOS provides for new hardware and software configurations through the use of a file called CONFIG.SYS. Using a series of special DOS commands, which make up the contents of CONFIG.SYS, you can easily establish the hardware/software relationships required by new hardware or application software. In fact, it is only through the CONFIG.SYS file that these commands can be executed.

When you start or restart your computer, the first action taking place is the reading of the BIOS (Basic Input/Output and Disk Operating System) and DOS files. These files are called **hidden files** because they are on your system disk, but are not displayed as part of the disk directory. The contents of these hidden files are copyrighted. They contain a detailed description of your system's input and output requirements along with disk operating system procedures that the processor needs for normal operations.

After BIOS.COM and DOS.COM are loaded into memory, DOS defaults to the \ (root) directory and looks for a CONFIG.SYS file. If the configuration file is present, DOS then loads it into memory and executes every command in the file, one after another. This is called **batch processing** because all the commands reside in one file and can immediately be processed together as a group, or batch. It is CONFIG.SYS that defines special software or hardware options that are not identified by the BIOS. Figure 7.1 illustrates the internal booting procedures described here.

CONFIGURATION COMMANDS

The best way to explain these software and hardware options is through a review of the configuration commands. Then, you will learn how to customize CONFIG.SYS for personal use.

BREAK (Default is OFF)

This command defines when DOS will check to see if the Control + Break key combination has been pressed. Pressing this two-key sequence indicates that the user wants to stop the current computer activity (see Chapter 2 for more details). In the default condition (OFF), DOS will check for a Ctrl + Break keypress during keyboard reading and screen or printer writing. When the BREAK is set ON, DOS will check for the Ctrl + Break keypress during all input/output operations, including disk access. The standard syntax for the BREAK command is as follows:

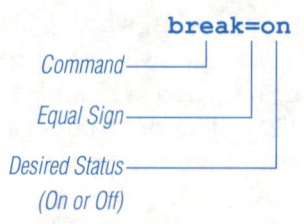

```
                        break=on
        Command ────────┘  │  │
      Equal Sign ──────────┘  │
   Desired Status ────────────┘
      (On or Off)
```

The desired status of the BREAK option depends on your need for data protection. Since lost clusters and other problems result from unexpected

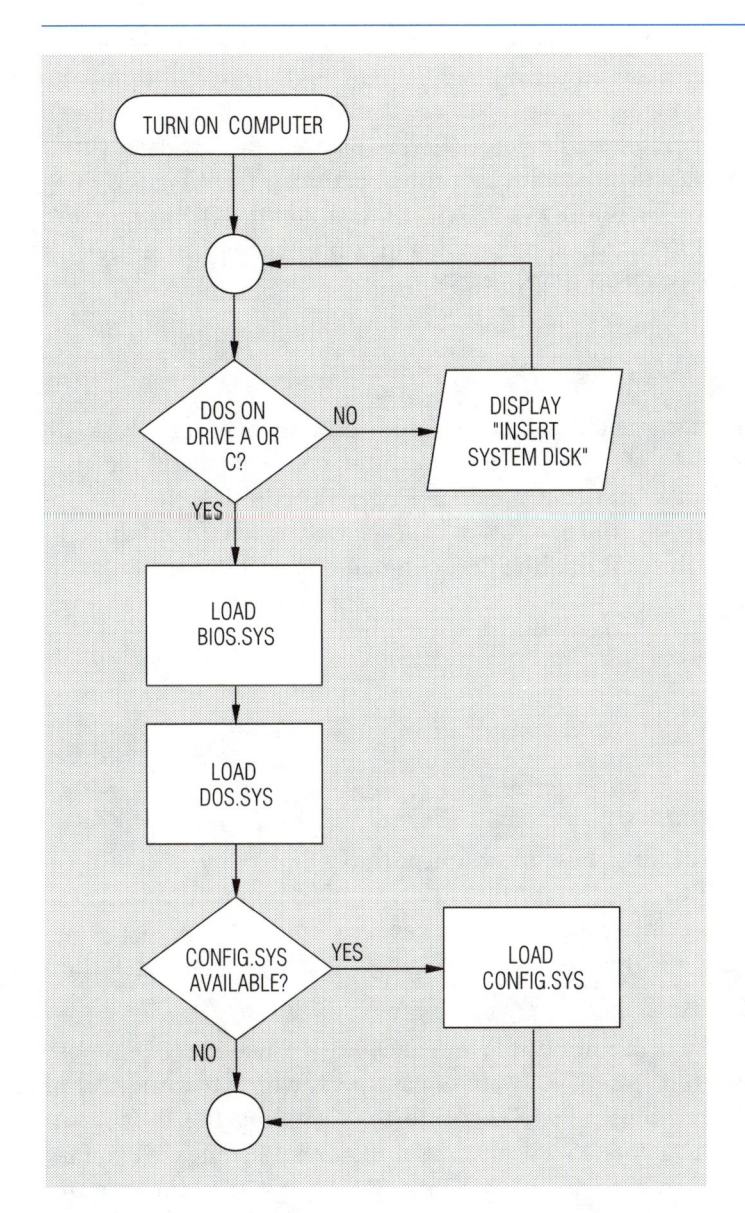

Figure 7.1
Internal booting procedures (Step 1).

termination of disk input and output, data protection is many times best accomplished by preventing you from interrupting disk input and output. This explains why the default state is BREAK OFF. In fact, data protection is so important that it is not uncommon for application software to set the BREAK OFF prior to execution.

NOTE: Setting the BREAK status can be accomplished without rebooting, through the DOS internal BREAK command, which functions identically to the configuration BREAK ON or OFF.

Typically there are two situations in which it may be advantageous to have the BREAK ON. First, if you are a programmer, it may be desirable to terminate execution at any point during program testing. The other situation would be if you are in the process of learning a new software package. In this case, Ctrl + Break may be a means to abort an unwanted action. In both cases it is recommended that you use the DOS BREAK command at the DOS prompt to temporarily change BREAK to ON, rather than making a change in the default setting by setting BREAK ON in CONFIG.SYS.

BUFFERS *(Default is 2)*

This BUFFERS command enables you to define how many work areas are added to DOS's normal data work area. It is through these special memory areas (***buffers***) that data temporarily reside during disk activities. Not only are data passed through these buffers, but the most recently read data are held in them. The standard syntax for the BUFFER command is as follows:

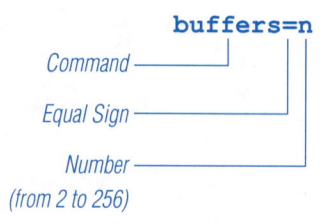

```
                    buffers=n
     Command ─────────┘ │ │
     Equal Sign ──────────┘ │
     Number ────────────────┘
   (from 2 to 256)
```

The use of buffers during disk input/output explains why many DOS commands, such as DIR, do not reread the disk when the command is executed twice. Assuming there is enough buffer space to hold all the requested information, DOS simply rereads this information from the input buffer. Repeated commands are executed much faster as a result.

The performance of the computer can be enhanced by increasing the number of active buffers. Programs such as database managers, which require a lot of disk access, benefit the most. The downside to increasing the number of buffers comes from two factors. First, each buffer requires 528 bytes of memory and provides 512 bytes of transfer space. Thus BUFFERS=20, would require 10K (1K = 1024 bytes) of memory. Second, if a very large number of buffers is allocated, it may take DOS longer to search the buffers for data than to physically read it from the disk. In most cases the accompanying software documentation will indicate the optimal setting.

NOTE: *If you are using a variety of software packages it will be necessary to set the BUFFERS equal to the largest value required.*

DOS experts recommend the following settings when none are otherwise specified:

IBM PC & XT or PS/2 25 or 30	10 to 20 buffers
IBM AT or PS/2 50, 60 or 80	10 to 30 buffers

FILES *(Default is 8)*

FILES is used to define the total number of files that can be opened by application software at the same time. In allocating files it is extremely important that you have an understanding of both your hardware and software needs. At start-up, DOS will need a minimum of three files for the keyboard (standard input), screen (standard temporary output) and printer (standard permanent output). The form for the FILES command is outlined below:

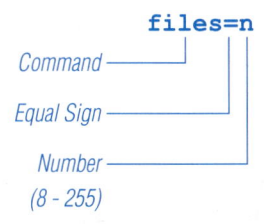

```
            files=n
Command ─────┘  │ │
Equal Sign ─────┘ │
Number ───────────┘
(8 - 255)
```

For example, if you have a mouse connected to your serial port (COM1:), then DOS will need a fourth file. As with buffers, memory (48 bytes) is set aside for every allocated file. The following table illustrates the file requirement for a standard personal computer system.

Hardware	Files	Definition
Keyboard	1	Standard input (part of CON:)
Screen	1	Standard output (part of CON:)
Printer	1	Standard printer (PRN:, LPT1:, LPT2: or LPT3:)
Mouse	1	Standard auxiliary (COM1: or COM2:)
ERRORLEVEL	1	Standard error (error handling in batch files)
Total	5	

This configuration would only leave three files for software use. In most cases this will be adequate. However, informed decisions require an understanding of software requirements. If your database or word processing programs can handle 10 open files, then you could not expect the default of 8 to work. In this case you would need set FILES=15 at a minimum. As with buffers, set the files to support the maximum number of files you would need for any of your software/hardware.

DEVICE

The DEVICE command enables you to configure your computer system to use special hardware. These devices require the loading of special drivers that handle communication between the system and the hardware. The basic syntax for the DEVICE command is outlined below:

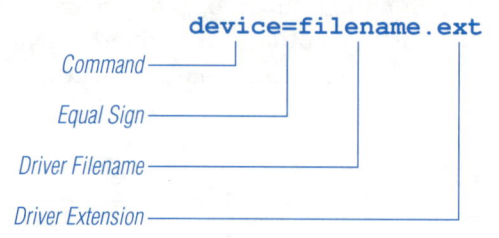

```
device=filename.ext
```
Command ─┘ │ │ │
Equal Sign ──┘ │ │
Driver Filename ──────┘ │
Driver Extension ───────────┘

The DEVICE command allows you to add to the standard input and output configuration defined by BIOS during booting. The following is a list of some typical devices you could install via the CONFIG.SYS file.

`device=ansi.sys`	Provides added features to the standard output (screen) some software requires.

`device=ramdrive.sys`
or
`device=vdisk.sys`
	Creates and drives special RAM (memory) disk that functions like a disk drive.

`device=mouse.sys`	Loads the driver for a mouse.
`device=hgc.sys`	Loads the driver for a monochrome graphics card.

NOTE: *Several of the device drivers listed above are furnished by the hardware manufacturer at the time of purchase and do not come with DOS.*

Most device drivers have a filename extension of .SYS. However, this extension is not required. Any number of device drivers could be loaded into memory using the device command. The computer's memory places the only practical limits on the number of devices you can install. It is usually suggested that all device drivers be listed in CONFIG.SYS in the order you want them loaded.

The best idea is to put them in the same place within CONFIG.SYS, one after the other.

NOTE: *The software drivers do not need to be located in the DOS root directory. If they are stored in a subdirectory, you must include the proper path (see Chapter 5: Hard Disk Management) with driver's filename.*

DRIVPARM

This command permits you to define new options (parameters) for device drivers that override the original defaults. You may find it necessary to use this command if you install hardware that has special abilities beyond the DOS defaults. The standard format for the DRIVPARM command is as follows:

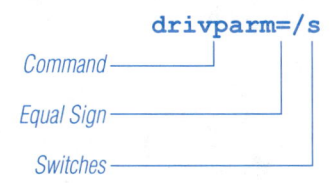

```
drivparm=/s
```

Command ─
Equal Sign ─
Switches ─

One common application for DRIVPARM occurs when people are installing 3-1/2 inch disk drives in their personal computers. If you had a 3-1/2 inch drive as drive B you would need the following DRIVPARM command in your configuration file.

```
drivparm=/d:1 /f:2
```

This command tells DOS that device 1 (0=A, 1=B, etc.) should be formatted at 720K. Without this command DOS would only format your 3-1/2 inch disks at 360K, the system default. Common drive parameters are listed below:

/d:n Identify drive (A=0, B=1, etc.)

/c   Specifies that door lock support is required

/f:n Specifies device type from indexes listed below:
  0 = 320/360K bytes
  1 = 1.2M bytes
  2 = 720K bytes
  3 = 8" single density
  4 = 8" double density
  5 = Hard Disk
  6 = Tape Drive
  7 = Other

/h:n   Maximum head number (1 to 99)

/n   Nonremovable block device

/s:n   Number of sectors per track (1 to 99)

/t:n   Number of tracks per side (1 to 999)

NOTE: *DRIVPARM is not available with PC-DOS.*

LASTDRIVE *(Default is E)*

LASTDRIVE informs DOS of the number of drives it should recognize. DOS is able to use 26 drives. The syntax for the LASTDRIVE command is outlined below:

```
lastdrive=L
```
Command ─── (lastdrive)
Equal Sign ─── (=)
Letter (A-Z) ─── (L)

The creation of virtual drives and the use of the SUBST utility may require the establishment of additional drive designations. These drive designations can be a combination of physical and virtual drives. A ***physical drive*** is a piece of hardware being used as intended, i.e., a floppy disk drive to store data on floppy disks. ***Virtual drives*** are hardware with temporary assignments. Memory acting like an additional disk is one example of a virtual drive (see DOS User's Manual for more information).

COUNTRY *(Default is 001)*

The COUNTRY command permits DOS to use the selected international standards for time, date, currency, and case conversions on input and output hardware. For example, international standards for writing the date September 30, 1990 could vary between 9-30-90, 30-9-90 and even 90-9-30. The basic format for the COUNTRY commands follows:

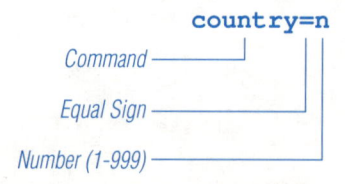

```
country=n
```
Command ─── (country)
Equal Sign ─── (=)
Number (1-999) ─── (n)

Common international conversions are listed below:

001	United States
031	Netherlands
032	Belgium
033	France
034	Spain
039	Italy
041	Switzerland
044	United Kingdom
045	Denmark
046	Sweden
047	Norway
049	Germany
061	Australia
358	Finland

FCBS *(Default is 4)*

FCBS permits you to determine the number of File Control Blocks that can be open concurrently. Some software packages use file control blocks as they work with data files. The standard syntax for the FCBS commands is shown below:

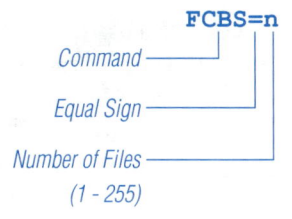

FCBS=n

- Command
- Equal Sign
- Number of Files (1 - 255)

SHELL

The SHELL command starts execution of the shell (command interpreter) from the specified file rather than the default COMMAND.COM. SHELL also identifies where COMMAND.COM is found when you relocate it from the root directory to a subdirectory. The general format for the SHELL command follows:

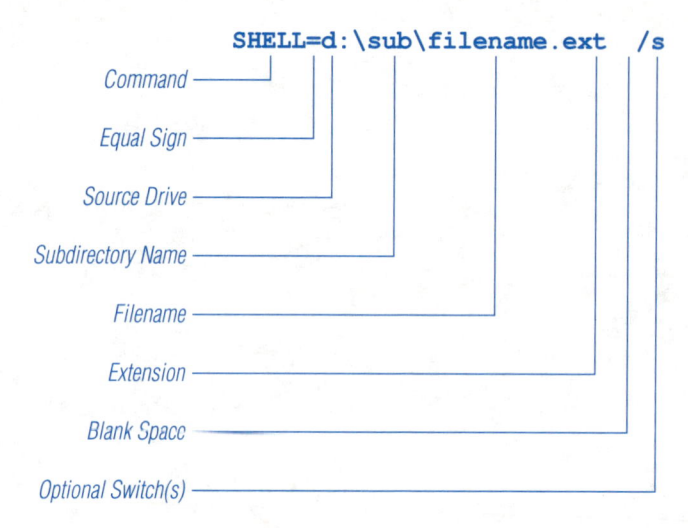

```
SHELL=d:\sub\filename.ext /s
```

- Command
- Equal Sign
- Source Drive
- Subdirectory Name
- Filename
- Extension
- Blank Space
- Optional Switch(s)

Two optional switches are available with the SHELL command:

/E The "environment" switch sets aside memory in the reserved memory area. For example, the switch /E:512 allocates 512 bytes of reserved memory for use by DOS.

/P The "protect" switch reserves a permanent area of memory for COMMAND.COM.

CREATING A CONFIG.SYS FILE

The easiest way to create a configuration file is with a word processor. Keep in mind that the file must be in a standard ASCII text. Check the word processing program's reference manual or use the TYPE command (see Problem 1 in Chapter 4: File Output) to make sure your word processor writes in ASCII code. Wordstar users, as an example, must create their CONFIG.SYS file in NONDOCUMENT mode.

Each command receives its own line in CONFIG.SYS, with spaces only used between switches. Be sure to save the file under the filename CONFIG.SYS. The file then should be copied into the system disk's root directory. The following screen shows a typical CONFIG.SYS file.

```
A>type config.sys ↵

files=24
buffers=20
device=ansi.sys
device=hgc.sys
device=mouse.sys
```

NOTE: *These commands can only be executed at startup. If you have made any changes to your configuration file, the system will have to be rebooted before they become active.*

EXPLORING DOS

1. What configuration command would you add to the CONFIG.SYS listed above if you wanted to use the currency symbol for a French Franc?

2. How would you use CONFIG.SYS to expand the number of active disk drives from the default of 5 to 7?

3. Your new printer came with a special device driver called PRINTPRO.SYS. What would you do to install this device driver?

CONFIG.SYS FILE ERRORS

Errors you make in an instruction line from CONFIG.SYS will not, in most cases, abort the booting process. DOS will usually display an error message on the screen as it continues to the next command in CONFIG.SYS. Typically, errors are in syntax (commands misspelled) or caused by the absence of specified device drivers. When errors occur, the configuration file needs to be corrected and the system restarted.

> ### DOS MESSAGES
>
> #### CONFIG.SYS
>
> **Unrecognized command in CONFIG.SYS**
>
> *You most likely have misspelled the configuration command, or possibly have used a standard DOS command. The DOS commands discussed in Chapters 1-6 do not execute from CONFIG.SYS.*
>
> **Bad or missing xxxx.SYS**
>
> *You have attempted to load a device driver, for example ANSI.SYS, but have incorrectly spelled the file name. The spelling you used is displayed in the DOS message and identified above as xxxx.SYS. However, if the spelling is correct, make sure the device driver is located in the root directory or that the correct subdirectory has been identified with the driver's filename.*

CUSTOMIZING SYSTEM OPERATIONS WITH AUTOEXEC.BAT

The batch processing principles used with CONFIG.SYS during booting can be independently employed by DOS users. The files that are created in this process end with a .BAT extension and are called **batch files**. DOS users can create a variety of batch files using any 8 characters in the filename (as long as they use a .BAT extension). In addition, DOS is designed to recognize and look for the AUTOEXEC.BAT file when booting.

Examine Figure 7.2 to review the booting process and to see where AUTOEXEC.BAT comes into the picture. After turning on the computer, the BIOS.COM, DOS.COM and CONFIG.SYS are read from the DOS disk to help DOS configure your system. Then COMMAND.COM is read from the DOS disk into memory to act as the system supervisor. The **command interpreter** (COMMAND.COM) is the internally active part of DOS that interacts with users. Internal DOS commands reside in COMMAND.COM. The DOS prompt is generated by the command interpreter, which also responds to DOS commands like DIR, COPY, DEL, etc.

Step 1

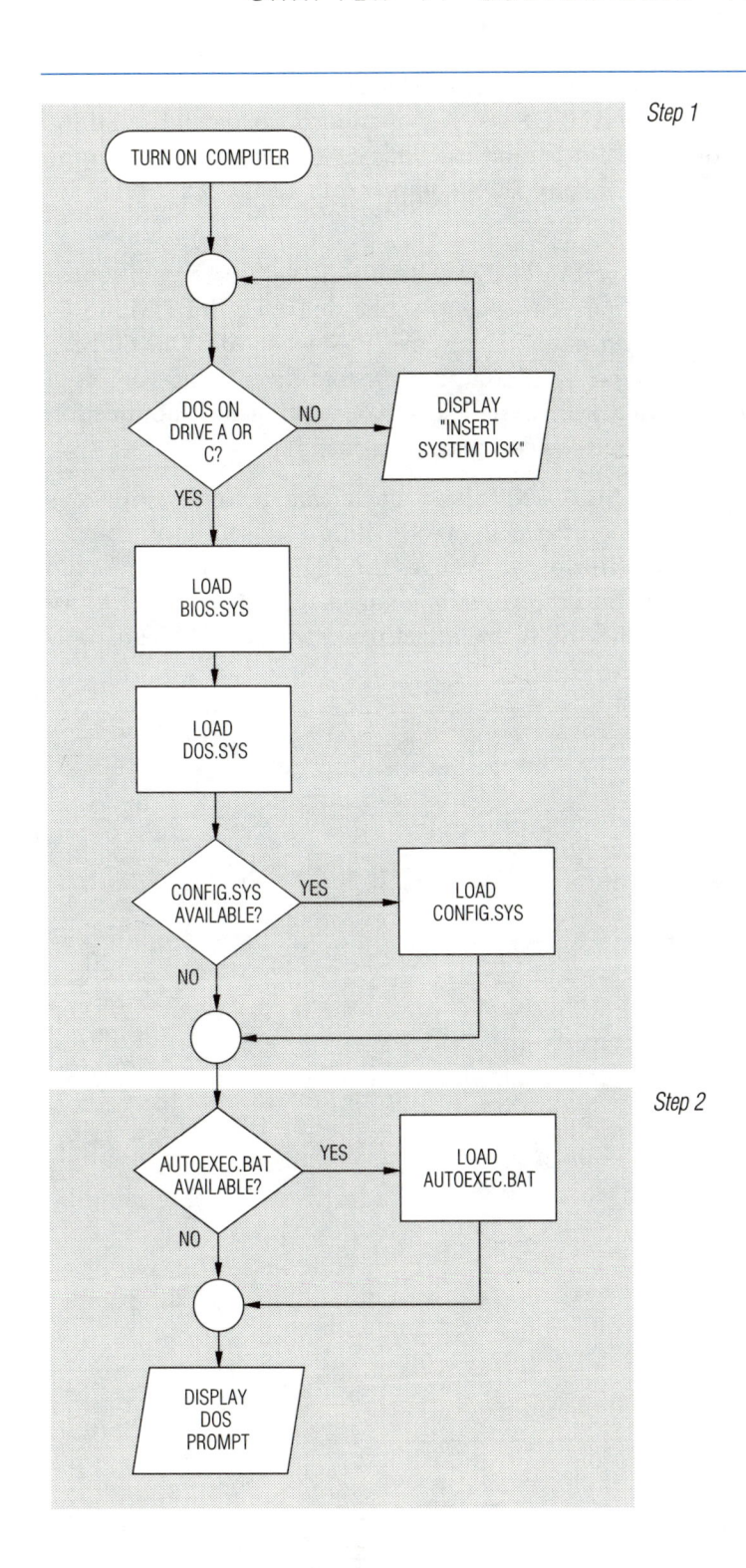

Figure 7.2
Internal booting procedures (Steps 1 and 2).

Step 2

Once the command interpreter is loaded, it checks the root directory of the boot disk for the presence of AUTOEXEC.BAT (autoexecute batch file). If the file is present, the command interpreter executes each DOS command in the file. The autoexec file can use any DOS command or utility acceptable for batch files.

While the commands used in AUTOEXEC.BAT will vary among personal computer configurations, in most cases people include DATE and TIME to set the date and time (which are not automatically executed when AUTOEXEC.BAT is present). You can customize your computer system by creating your own system prompt, establishing search paths, and executing any application software you want to run when the computer is turned on.

The next screen displays an AUTOEXEC.BAT that: clears the screen; executes the TIME and DATE commands; turns the verify option on; sets a search path back to the root and \DOS directories; changes the DOS prompt to show the current subdirectory; clears the screen again; changes the active subdirectory to \WORDPROC; and executes the WordPerfect word processing program.

```
C>type autoexec.bat ↵

cls
time
date
verify on
path c:\;c:\DOS
prompt $p$g
cls
cd c:\wordproc
wp
cd c:\
cls
```

After the above AUTOEXEC.BAT is executed during a system boot, the user will see WordPerfect's introductory display on the screen. When the user exits WordPerfect, DOS returns to the next instruction in AUTOEXEC.BAT. As a result, DOS moves back to the root directory and clears the screen before exiting AUTOEXEC.BAT and displaying the DOS prompt. Additional batch files are described in Appendix E: Practical Batch Files.

E X P L O R I N G   D O S

4. How would you change the preceding AUTOEXEC.BAT file if you wanted to customize the DOS prompt with your name?

5. How could you ask DOS to look for lost clusters every time you start up the system?

6. What additional command would you add to the AUTOEXEC.BAT if you wanted to let the user know which version of DOS was used by the computer system?

PROBLEM SOLVING WITH DOS

The purchase, installation, and automation of a new software package are the processes covered in this hands-on session. It involves customizing your system to use a new database management package.

The first step is to be sure of the hardware specifications. What follows are the primary specifications for a hypothetical system (you should know the same information about your own personal computer system):

Computer Type:	IBM PS/25
Main Memory:	640 bytes
Monitor:	Color with Enhanced Graphic Adapter (EGA) board
Disk Drives:	Drive A - 3-1/2 diskette
	Drive B - 3-1/2 diskette
	Drive C - Hard Disk with 40 megabytes of storage
DOS version:	MS-DOS 3.3
Printer:	Epson LX - 800

Now you are ready to ask some very important questions about the software you are considering.

- How much memory is required by the software? Will its operation be enhanced by having memory beyond the basic requirements?

- Does the software use graphics? If so, does it require a color monitor? Does it recognize and automatically configure for the monitor type available? If the software will run with a monochrome monitor, does it require a graphics card? If not, can it make use of one?

- Does the software require a hard disk drive? If not, how much is its efficiency improved by access to a hard disk? Can the software make use of active PATH settings?

- What is the earliest version of MS/PC-DOS that the software can use?

- Does the software generate printed reports? If so, will it configure for the manufacturer and model printer you have?

- Is the software copy protected?

CHAPTER 7: CUSTOMIZING YOUR SYSTEM

After asking these questions, assume now you have purchased the First Base File Manager. The specifications for the software are as follows:

- IBM (PC, XT, AT, PS/2) and compatibles
- Requires 512K Memory
- Will work with color and monochrome monitors, self-configuring. Performance improved with 20 buffers and access to ANSI.SYS screen driver (found on \DOS subdirectory)
- Supports 15 active files
- Works with Dual Floppies and hard disk drives (will handle DOS paths).
- Will configure to printer.
- Not copy protected.

PROBLEM 1

After backing up the First Base master disks, you will need to create subdirectories for the First Base software (DBM) and associated database files (FILES). The FILES subdirectory is subordinate to DBM, which is subordinate to the \SOFTWARE directory. This directory hierarchy is illustrated below:

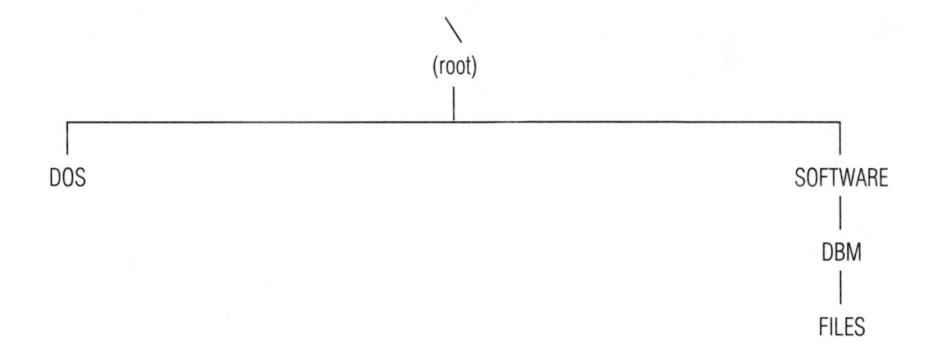

```
              \
           (root)
         ____|____
        |         |
       DOS     SOFTWARE
                  |
                 DBM
                  |
                FILES
```

Assuming that the \SOFTWARE directory already exists, what DOS commands would you use to create \SOFTWARE\DBM and \SOFTWARE\DBM\FILES, and to copy the contents of the First Base master in drive A to \SOFTWARE\DBM?

Answer:

```
C>md \software\dbm ↵
C>md \software\dbm\files ↵
C>copy a:*.* c:\software\dbm /v ↵
```

PROBLEM 2

Now that the software is loaded, turn your attention to the CONFIG.SYS file. How would you check to see if CONFIG.SYS already exists? Remember, CONFIG.SYS is usually found in the root directory.

Answer: *Display the root directory with: DIR C:\ /P*

PROBLEM 3

Suppose your hypothetical system does not have a CONFIG.SYS or AUTOEXEC.BAT in the root subdirectory. How would you create a new CONFIG.SYS and what DOS configuration commands would you include in the new CONFIG.SYS file?

Answer: *Use a word processing program that creates ASCII text files. An alternative would be to use the COPY command to duplicate typed DOS commands from the keyboard (CON) to a new CONFIG.SYS file as shown below:*

```
C>copy con c:\config.sys ↵
buffers=20 ↵
files=20 ↵
device=c:\dos\ansi.sys ↵
^z ↵          Press F6, then Enter.
```

CHAPTER 7: CUSTOMIZING YOUR SYSTEM 173

NOTE: *The DOS prompt will disappear until you press the F6 (or Ctrl + Z) and Enter keys. Pressing the F6 key places an end-of-file mark in CONFIG.SYS and terminates the COPY command. The file should be written to disk now. List the directory to confirm its presence and then TYPE the file to confirm accuracy. If there are any errors, re-enter.*

PROBLEM 4

Assume you already have a CONFIG.SYS file. In this situation you use the TYPE command to inspect its contents on the screen as shown below:

```
C>type config.sys ↵
files=15
buffers=24
```

How will you update CONFIG.SYS to reflect the optimum needs of the new database management program?

Answer: *You will be looking for the commands you need to have present for your new software. If these commands currently exist in CONFIG.SYS, then confirm that they are set at the needed levels. In this situation buffers=24, which exceeds the needs of First Base, so you leave it stand. On the other hand, files=15 does not meet First Base's optimum conditions for 20 open files. As a result, it should be changed to files=20. In addition, access to ANSI.SYS is desirable and device=c:\dos\ansi.sys should be added to CONFIG.SYS.*

You should not erase the original CONFIG.SYS, but use it as a backup by following the procedures outlined below:

1. *Use the COPY command to make a duplicate file called CONFIG.TMP.*
2. *Load your word processor and configure it for non-document or ASCII mode if necessary.*
3. *Load config.tmp into your word processor and make the changes necessary.*
4. *Save the file and exit from the wordprocessor.*
5. *Rename CONFIG.SYS to CONFIG.BUP*
6. *Rename CONFIG.TMP to CONFIG.SYS*

You now have the updated CONFIG.SYS file, yet have retained the original (CONFIG.BUP) should there be any problems. The final step is to warm boot (reset) your computer, since the configuration you desire will not be active until you do. From this point forth, the desired configuration will be set at startup.

WARNING

It is becoming a common practice for software publishers to include automated setup utilities with their software. These utilities will, if the software requires, check for the existence of CONFIG.SYS and possibly AUTOEXEC.BAT. If the file(s) are not present, the utility will create them with the required commands as part of the software installation. Should the file(s) exist, the utility will add what it needs to the existing file(s). In this situation a potential problem comes into play. Remember your CONFIG.SYS file that existed at the start of this problem contained a buffers=24 command. It is possible that an automated set-up utility would modify the file as follows:

```
files=15
buffers=24
files=20
buffers=20
```

DOS will configure on the last encountered command in CONFIG.SYS should there be duplicate commands. This, of course, does not apply to commands such as device= or drivparm= assuming these commands load different drivers or establish parameters for different drives.

The end result of the CONFIG.SYS command above is that the buffers setting has been reduced. Since First Base does not require 24 buffers, the automatic changes made by this new software's installation procedures will not cause problems. The changed setting could cause problems with other software that may have higher buffer requirements or reduce overall computer performance.

PROBLEM 5

To complete the customization of your system to the new software you need to create an autoexecute batch file (AUTOEXEC.BAT). What DOS commands would you include in this batch file?

Answer: While there are several correct answers, these DOS commands are recommended in this situation:

DATE	*Will not be automatic when using AUTOEXEC.BAT.*
TIME	*Will not be automatic when using AUTOEXEC.BAT.*
VERIFY ON	*Check all disk I/O*
PATH=C:\;C:\DOS	*Set a search path to root and \DOS directories*
PROMPT PG	*Include active subdirectory and > in prompt*

PROBLEM 6

Since batch files help customize your system as well as make it easier to use, you should create a \BATCH subdirectory to store various .BAT files. Furthermore, you can customize your system by creating a batch file that automatically changes the active subdirectory to \SOFTWARE\DBM and starts execution of the First Base File Manager by typing FIRSTBAS at the DOS prompt. How would you go about creating a \BATCH subdirectory and the FIRSTBAS.BAT batch file?

Answer: Type md \batch to create the \BATCH subdirectory and use your word processing software or COPY CON (see Problem 3) to create FIRST.BAT with the following DOS commands:

```
cd c:\software\dbm ↵
firstbas ↵
cd c:\ ↵
```

PROBLEM 7

You are now ready to try your new batch file FIRST.BAT which resides in \BATCH. The screen below shows the result of your first attempt to use FIRST.BAT. What went wrong?

```
C:\>first ↵
Bad command or file name
```

Answer: Since FIRST.BAT is not in the root directory, which is the active subdirectory (look at the DOS prompt), DOS cannot execute the commands in this batch program. Either identify where to find FIRST.BAT in the command line by entering:

> C:\>\batch\first ↵

or add \BATCH to the search path with:

> C:\>path \;\dos;\batch ↵

EXPLORING DOS ANSWERS

1. COUNTRY=33

2. Add **lastdriv=g** to CONFIG.SYS.

3. Add **device=printpro.sys** to CONFIG.SYS.

4. Delete the current PROMPT instruction and replace it with **PROMPT (your name)$g**.

5. Add **CHKDSK /F** to the AUTOEXEC.BAT

6. Add **VER** to the beginning or end of AUTOEXEC.BAT.

8
What's New with DOS 4.0

IN THIS CHAPTER:

MEM
SECLECT
SHELL
SWITCHES

In the second decade of personal computing many people find themselves working with microcomputers. As we gain skill with these new tools, expectations and needs expand with experience.

Computer users can now choose from a wide range of software packages that combine text, numbers, graphics, and scanned images to produce finished products. In turn, the needs of personal computer (PC) users rise to meet and challenge each new enchancement to application software that programmers can offer.

MS/PC DOS has responded to this increased sophistication of users and software by regularly enhancing DOS, from version 1.0 through 4.0. Upgrading to a newer version of the Disk Operating System is a formidable task for both Microsoft/IBM and the user. At some point, old ideas and ways of doing things must be set aside. In this chapter you will examine new instructions and enhancements to existing instructions brought about by 4.0.

Expansion of PC applications has resulted in increased memory requirements by software and the need for more disk space. The original limits imposed by DOS on conventional memory at 640K have become a barrier. Furthermore, some users have bumped against the limits DOS places on disk space. Versions 3.3 and earlier could use up to, but not exceed, 32M of space on a hard disk.

SPECIAL DOS 4.0 FEATURES

The first DOS 4.0 feature users confront is the SELECT program, which creates a working system disk or "startup" disk. The SELECT program is executed as part of the AUTOEXEC.BAT file on the INSTALL disk. SELECT uses interactive queries concerning default parameters you wish to use with the system. A minimum of 256K memory is required to install DOS 4.0.

DOS MESSAGES

SELECT

Incorrect DOS Version

You have tried to use the SELECT program with an earlier version of DOS. Type VER to identify the current version of DOS running on your system and restart your system using a compatible DOS version.

```
Invalid Parameters on SELECT Command Line
Make sure the INSTALL diskette is in drive A:,
then press Ctrl + Alt + Del to restart
```

If the INSTALL diskette is in drive A, you can avoid restarting your system by executing the SELECT program from the instruction line using the MENU parameter, i.e., type SELECT MENU and then press the Enter key.

```
Invalid SELECT Boot Media
Insert the INSTALL diskette in drive A:, then retry
```

The SELECT program is on the DOS INSTALL disk, which must be in drive A. Make sure you are using the correct disk and try restarting the system again.

```
Invalid Disk/Diskette Media
Insert the INSTALL diskette in drive a:, then retry
```

The SELECT program is on the DOS INSTALL disk, which must be in drive A. If you are installing a system that uses a hard disk, you will still need to start-up and execute the SELECT program from drive A. Hard disk users only need to install once.

EXTENDED AND EXPANDED MEMORY

Many of the "new" DOS features found in version 4.0 have been available with third-party DOS support packages. Expanded and extended memory that allow users to access more that 640K main memory is a case in point. New device drivers, XMA2EMS.SYS and XMAEM.SYS, provide DOS with access to expanded memory. Now that these device drivers are available with DOS it is easier to enhance operations by saving space in main memory.

The difference between extended and expanded memory is rather technical. Basically, **extended memory** is hardware-specific memory with set internal address. It "extends" memory from a range of 1M to 16M. On the other hand, **expanded memory** is referenced by applications software that is designed to use additional memory beyond the 640K limit.

WORD-ORIENTED SHELL

The addition of a word-oriented shell is another example of DOS 4.0 incorporating features that users once had to purchase from third-party vendors. A **shell** works like a sophisticated menu. It displays DOS options to users and lets them select the command or utility (with switches) they wish to use.

There are two parts to the DOS shell: Start Programs and File System. The main menus of these two parts are shown in Figures 8.1 and 8.2. The Start Programs menu allows you to execute internal commands and external utilities and to change the colors DOS uses with screen displays. From the File System, you can view, manipulate, and execute application programs. Users can use the File System to highlight selected files for copying, deleting, or moving.

Once again, DOS has shown it must be responsive to users who work within an integrated personal computing environment. Inclusion of a DOS shell is the result of increased demand by users for a user-friendly disk operating system. You execute DOS commands and utilities from within the shell by moving the cursor to the desired option and pressing the Enter key. The shell will then walk you through the proper instruction syntax. Situations which call for using wild card characters (* and ?) can be executed from the shell as easily as they are from the instruction line. However, shells do not reduce your need to understand DOS instructions. What it does is provide you with visual prompts regarding the proper DOS syntax. Thus, as shown in Figure 8.3, the shell acts as an interface between the user and DOS.

Figure 8.1
Main menu of DOS shell's Start Programs.

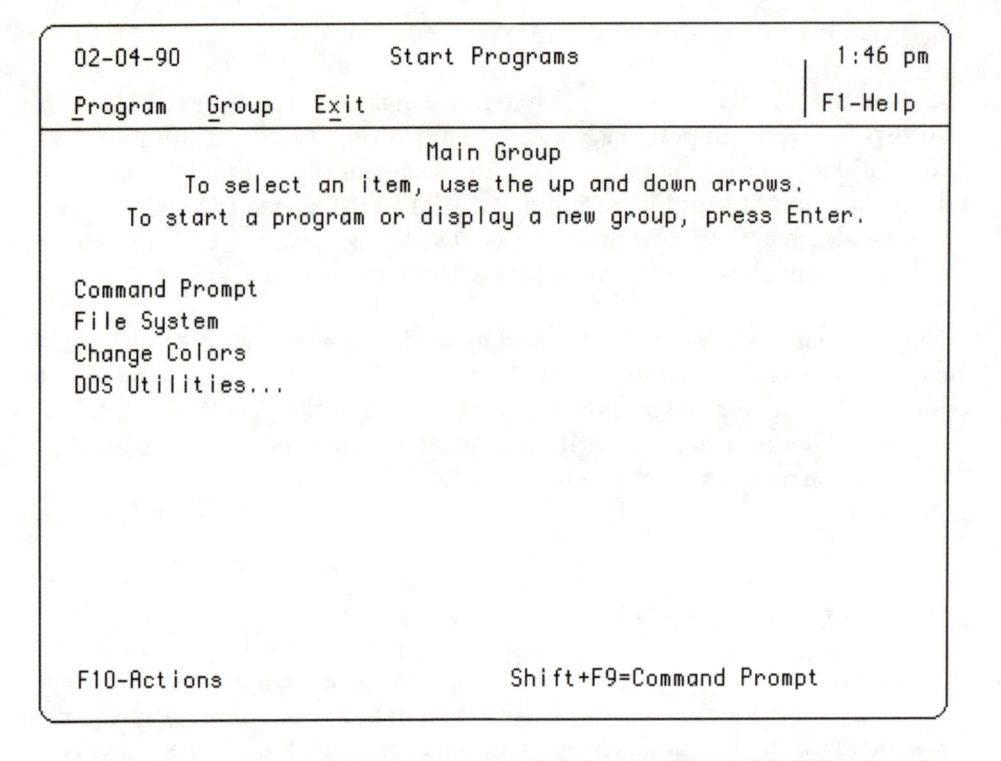

```
02-04-90                  Start Programs                    1:46 pm
Program   Group   Exit                                      F1-Help
─────────────────────────────────────────────────────────────────────
                              Main Group
              To select an item, use the up and down arrows.
          To start a program or display a new group, press Enter.


    Command Prompt
    File System
    Change Colors
    DOS Utilities...








    F10-Actions                    Shift+F9=Command Prompt
```

Figure 8.2
Main menu of DOS shell's File System.

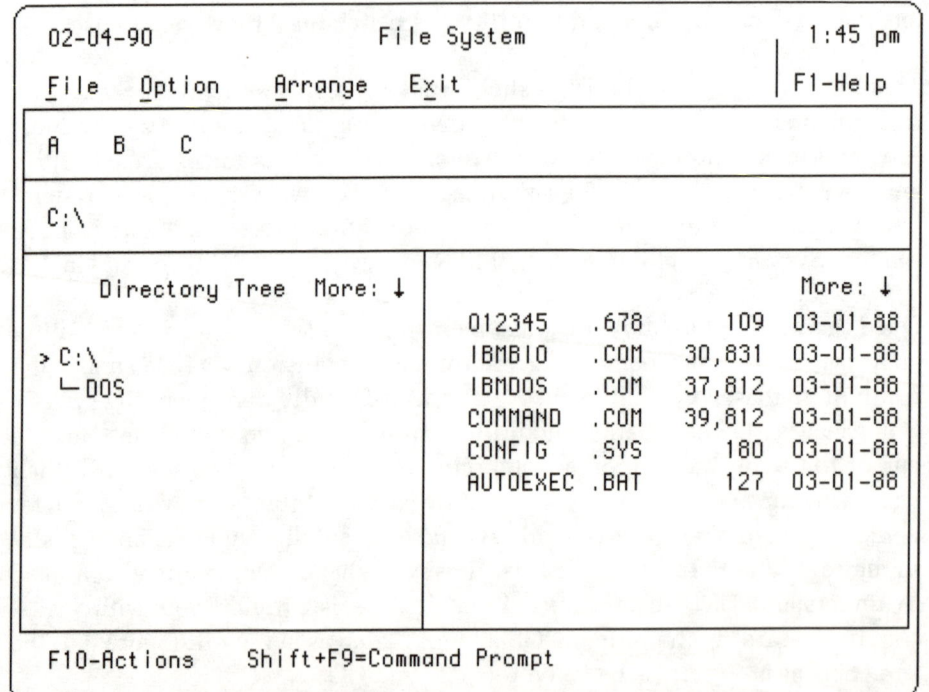

```
02-04-90                    File System                      1:45 pm
File   Option   Arrange   Exit                              F1-Help
─────────────────────────────────────────────────────────────────────
 A    B    C
─────────────────────────────────────────────────────────────────────
 C:\

         Directory Tree   More: ↓                           More: ↓
                                    012345    .678      109  03-01-88
    > C:\                           IBMBIO    .COM   30,831  03-01-88
       └ DOS                        IBMDOS    .COM   37,812  03-01-88
                                    COMMAND   .COM   39,812  03-01-88
                                    CONFIG    .SYS      180  03-01-88
                                    AUTOEXEC  .BAT      127  03-01-88




    F10-Actions     Shift+F9=Command Prompt
```

Figure 8.3
DOS shell acts as an interface between the user and DOS

NEW COMMANDS AND UTILITIES

DOS 4.0 includes several new commands and utilities. Included in this section is a brief overview of those new instructions that are of immediate use to average DOS users.

MEM

The external MEM utility provides a status report similar to CHKDSK. The standard syntax for MEM is as follows:

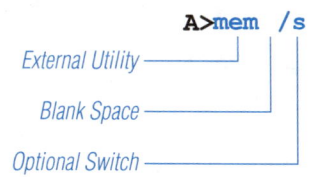

```
              A>mem /s
External Utility ─┘  │ │
    Blank Space ─────┘ │
Optional Switch ───────┘
```

There is really little difference between the status report provided by MEM and CHKDSK. However, additional information is supplied with the /PROGRAM switch which displays a status report of the current memory addresses of resident programs. When extended memory is available, the MEM /PROGRAM status report displays information about extended memory when device drivers are installed.

NOTE: DOS 4.0 requires the use of the full word "program" for switches associated with MEM.

To display the current status of memory.

```
A>mem ↵

655360 bytes total memory
655360 bytes available
587504 largest executable program size
```

To display the current status of memory and resident programs using MEM and the /Program switch.

```
A>mem /program ↵

Address    Name      Size      Type
--------   --------  --------  --------
000000               000400    Interrupt Vector
000400               000100    ROM Communication Area
000500               000200    DOS Communication Area

000700     IBMBIO    002470    System Program

002B70     IBMDOS    008880    System Program

00B3F0     IBMBIO    003F00    System Data
           ANSI      001190      DEVICE=
```

```
                    0000C0     FILES=
                    000100     FCBS=
                    0029A0     BUFFERS=
                    0001C0     LASTDRIV=
 00F300   COMMAND   001A20     Program
    .        .         .          .
    .        .         .          .
    .        .         .          .

 655360 bytes total memory
 655360 bytes available
 580736 largest executable program size
```

Extended DOS Messages

Changes have also been made to some of the configuration commands. One of the most important changes users should be aware of concerns the handling of DOS messages. The complete syntax for DOS messages are accessed by the command interpreter (COMMAND.COM) from disk when needed, just like external utility programs. If the command interpreter is not available the abbreviated messages **Extended Error X** or **Parse Error X** will appear (see DOS Message Box for list of error codes).

The complete syntax for extended DOS messages can be stored in memory by using the SHELL configuration command with /MSG and /P switches. This entry would appear in CONFIG.SYS as follows:

> **SHELL=A:\COMMAND.COM /MSG /P**

When this option is used, DOS displays a complete error message even when COMMAND.COM is not available. New users working on systems without hard disks would benefit from having the extended DOS messages resident in memory. The reason is that floppy disk users often have to remove the DOS disk from the default drive when using other software packages. Hard disk users do not have to worry because COMMAND.COM is always available on the root directory.

DOS message displayed when DOS locates COMMAND.COM, or when /MSG and /P are used in CONFIG.SYS within SHELL command.

```
A>dir /x ↵
invalid switch -   /x
```

DOS message displayed when DOS cannot find COMMAND.COM, and /MSG and /P are not used in CONFIG.SYS.

```
A>dir /x ↵
Parse Error 3
```

DOS MESSAGES

Error Codes

Extended Error x

DOS cannot find the command interpreter (COMMAND.COM) and therefore cannot access the extended DOS messages. Interpretations for the error code follow:

1	Invalid function	13	Invalid data
2	File not found	15	Invalid drive specification
3	Path not found	16	Attempt to remove current directory
4	Too many open files		
5	Access denied	17	Not same device
6	Invalid handle	18	No more files
7	Memory control blocks destroyed	19	Write-protect error
		20	Invalid unit
8	Insufficient memory	21	Not ready
9	Invalid memory block address	22	Invalid device request
		23	Data error
10	Invalid environment	24	Invalid device request parameters
11	Invalid format		
12	Invalid function parameter	25	Seek error

26	Invalid media type	39	Insufficient disk space
27	Sector not found	80	File exists
28	Printer out of paper error	82	Cannot make directory entry
29	Write fault error	83	Fail on INT 24
30	Read fault error	84	Too many redirections
31	General failure	85	Duplicate redirection
32	Sharing violation	86	Invalid password
33	Lock violation	87	Invalid parameter
34	Invalid disk change	88	Network data fault
35	FCB unavailable	90	Required system component not installed
36	System resource exhausted		
38	Out of input		

Parse Error x

DOS cannot find the command interpreter (COMMAND.COM) and therefore cannot access the extended DOS messages. Interpretations for the error code follow:

1	Too many parameters
2	Required parameter missing
3	Invalid switch
4	Invalid keyword
6	Parameter value not in allowed range
7	Parameter value not allowed
8	Parameter value not allowed
9	Parameter format not correct
10	Invalid parameter
11	Invalid parameter combination

SWITCHES=/K

The SWITCHES command with the /K "conventional Keyboard" switch allows compatibility for applications that do not support the expanded keyboard. When this command is included in CONFIG.SYS, DOS will respond to an enhanced keyboard as if it where a conventional XT or AT keyboard (see Chapter 2 for examples of these keyboards).

CHANGES TO FAMILIAR COMMANDS AND UTILITIES

Some of the existing commands and utilities have undergone minor enhancements. The following is a review of those instructions you are likely to be using.

BACKUP

The backup utility program with DOS 4.0 will now automatically format a new target disk if it is not already formatted.

To backup files to an unformatted target disk in drive B:

```
C>backup a: b: /s ↵

  Insert backup source diskette in drive A:
  Press any key to continue . . .


  Insert backup diskette 01 in drive B:

  WARNING! Files in the target drive B:\ root directory
  will be erased
  Press any key to continue . . .
  xx percent of disk formatted


  Format complete

  362496 bytes total disk space
  362496 bytes available

     1024 bytes in each allocation unit
      354 allocation units available on disk

  Volume Serial Number is 3559-13D0


  Format another (Y/N)?n ↵


  *** Backing up files to drive b: ***
```

```
    Diskette Number: 01

    \ANAL89.RPT        .        .
          .    .
          .    .
```
The entire disk, including subdirectories, are backed up on target disk.

DEL (ERASE)

The new /P "prompt" switch will ask the user to confirm file deletion. This switch is particularly useful when used in conjunction with wild card characters.

```
    A>del *.doc /p ↵

    A:\ANNUAL89.DOC,       Delete (Y/N)?_
```
DOS prompts user before deleting each file.

FORMAT

The FORMAT utility now automatically asks the user for a volume label. Users can employ the /V: "volume" switch to add the desired volume label (up to 11 characters) as part of the instruction line. This eliminates the need for DOS to prompt entering the label. DOS also displays to the user the percentage of space currently initialized as it formats the new disk.

The new /F "format size" switch makes it easier to format a removable disk at less then default capacity of the disk drive. For example, in a 3-1/2 inch, 1.44M disk drive you could format a diskette at 720K with the FORMAT /F:720 instruction. While other combinations are possible, the other practical application of the /F switch occurs when you need to format a 5-1/4 inch floppy disk at 360K in a 1.2M high capacity disk drive.

After formatting is complete, DOS displays the standard messages that indicate the total disk space and bytes of storage available on the disk. In addition, the number of bytes in each allocation unit, the total number of allocation units on the disk, and a volume serial number have been added to the screen display. The serial number is generated by DOS.

```
C>format a: /v:work disk ↵

Insert new diskette for drive A:
and press ENTER when ready...

xx percent of disk formatted

Format complete

362496 bytes total disk space
362496 bytes available on disk

  1024 bytes in each allocation unit
   354 allocation units available on disk

Volume Serial Number is 3E5C-19F2

Format another (Y/N)?_
```

REPLACE

The 4.0 PC-DOS REPLACE utility now has a /U "update" switch that works the same as the MS-DOS /D "date" switch. This switch allows you to replace files based on the most current date.

TIME

The system TIME can now be entered as a 24-hour or 12-hour clock. The COUNTRY command used in CONFIG.SYS determines which clock entry to use. When entering the time for a 12-hour clock, you must enter either an a (a.m.) or p (p.m.), for example, 9:30p for 9:30 p.m. The U.S. default is a 12-hour clock.

```
A>time ↵

Current time is  7:11:08.53p
Enter new time:_
```

Minor changes have been made to these commands and utilities:
- APPEND
- CHKDSK
- MODE
- SYS

CHANGES TO CONFIGURATION COMMANDS

DOS 4.0 introduces some enhancements to the configuration commands. The following is a brief description of the changes users can expect to find.

BUFFERS

DOS 4.0 will allow BUFFERS configured with the system to read and write data at a faster rate. As a result, DOS can utilize more buffers with greater efficiency. Furthermore, buffers can be kept in expanded memory by including the /X "eXpanded memory" switch.

COUNTRY

The COUNTRY command now supports the following:

081	Japan
082	Korea
086	Simplified Chinese
088	Traditional Chinese

Minor changes have been made to these device drivers:

ANSI.SYS

DISPLAY.SYS

PRINTER.SYS

WHAT'S NEXT?

The word-oriented DOS shell is just the beginning. You can expect to see a graphics shell, called the presentation manager. A **presentation manager** identifies DOS commands and utilities through the use of *icons*, or pictures, which represent the desired action. For example, instead of typing DEL to erase a file, you could use a mouse to point at the filename and then an icon of a trash can to delete the file.

Microsoft and IBM are now supporting OS/2 which is a new microcomputer-based disk operating system. OS/2 is **multi-tasking**, which means it can run several programs concurrently. You may think this is the end-of-the-line for DOS. But this is not the case. OS/2 will work with DOS. In this situation, programs designed to work with DOS can be executed from OS/2.

Appendix A

DISK DRIVES AND MEDIA

It pays to familiarize yourself with storage media. IBM and IBM-compatible microcomputers use 5-1/4 inch floppy disks and 3-1/2 inch diskettes. The storage capacity and means for protecting data will vary among disk types.

5-1/4 INCH FLOPPY DISKS

Figure A.1 illustrates the critical elements of a 5-1/4 inch floppy disk. When the ***write-protect notch*** is covered, data can be read (input) from the disk but not written (output) to it.

Disk drives designed to use 5-1/4 inch floppy disks have a variety of mechanisms for opening and closing the disk drive door. Two of the more common types of disk drives are shown in Figure A.2.

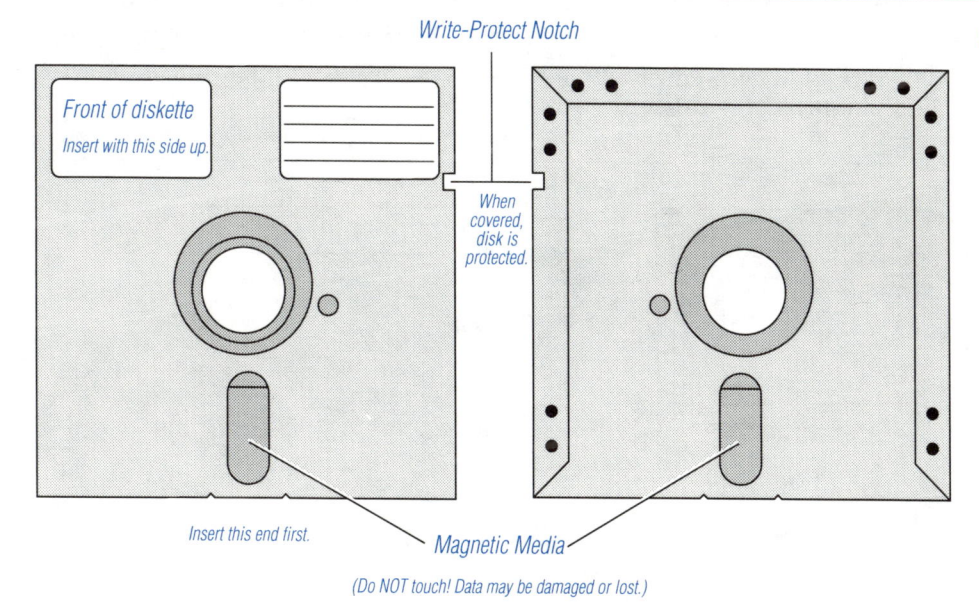

Figure A.1
5-1/4 inch floppy disk.

Figure A.2
Typical disk drives for 5-1/4 inch floppy disks

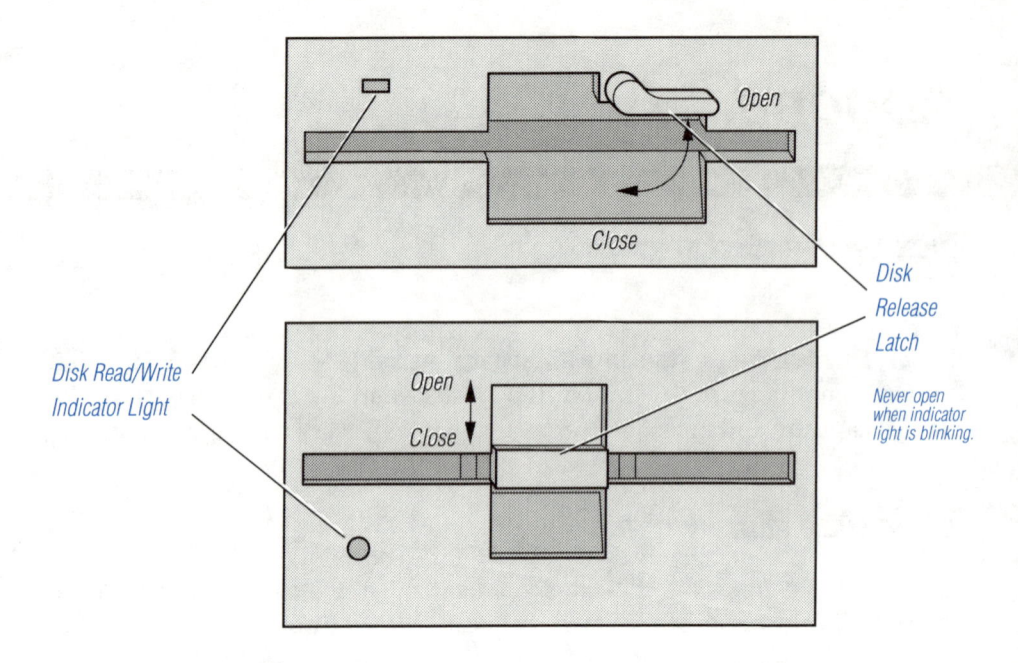

3-1/2 INCH DISKETTES

The 3-1/2 inch diskette shown in Figure A.3 has grown in popularity and appears destined to replace the 5-1/4 inch floppy disk, since it holds more data while being smaller in size. Furthermore, these disks are less vulnerable than 5-1/4 inch floppy disks because of their hard plastic case and metal shutter. Data on 3-1/2 disks are protected from accidental erasure by opening the **write-protect window** shown in Figure A.3.

Figure A.3
3-1/2 inch diskette.

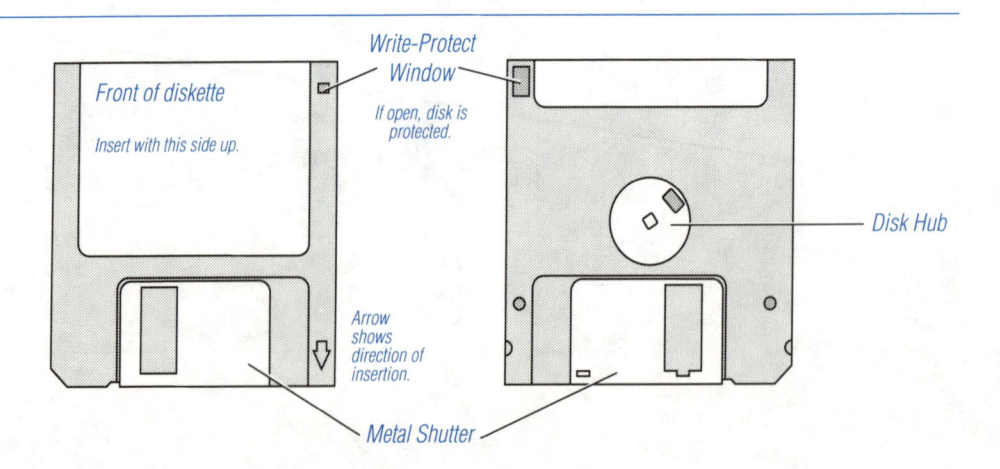

APPENDIX B **193**

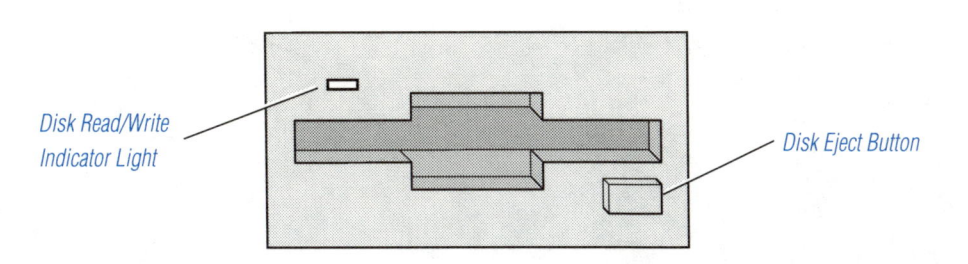

Figure A.4
Typical diskette drive for a 3-1/2 inch diskette.

Load 3-1/2 inch diskettes into the disk drive by firmly pushing the diskette into the opening until it drops and locks into place. Figure A.4 shows the disk eject button on the 3-1/2 inch diskette drive that users press to remove the diskette.

A comparison of the storage capacity of standard 5-1/4 inch floppy disks and 3-1/2 inch diskettes is provided in Figure A.5.

ORGANIZATION AND LAYOUT OF DISK MEDIA

The floppy disks and diskettes used by IBM and IBM-compatible computers are soft-sectored. As shown in Figure A.6, **soft-sectored** disks have a single sensing hole that the disk drive uses for orientation.

When a new disk is formatted, DOS creates a series of concentric **tracks** and subdivides the tracks into **sectors** (see Figure A.7). The sensing hole found on soft-sectored disks identifies the beginning of each track. After establishing the tracks and sectors, DOS sets aside the first track for the disk directory and file allocation table (FAT).

Dimensions	5-1/4"	5-1/4"	3-1/2"	3-1/2"
Density	Double	High	Double	High
Number of Tracks	40	80	80	80
Number of Sectors	9	15	9	18
Characters per Sector	512	512	512	512
Maximum Directory Entries	112	224	112	224
Total characters per disk	360K	1.2M	720K	1.44M

Figure A.5
Comparison of removable disk media.

Figure A.6
The sensing hole found on a soft-sectored disk identifies the beginning of each track.

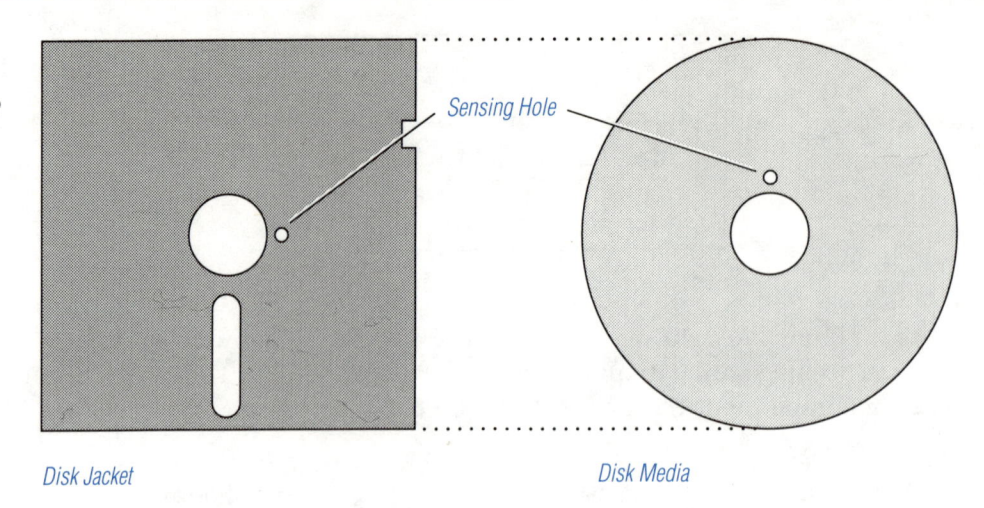

Sensing Hole

Disk Jacket

Disk Media

Figure A.7
Data stored on disks is arranged into tracks and sectors.

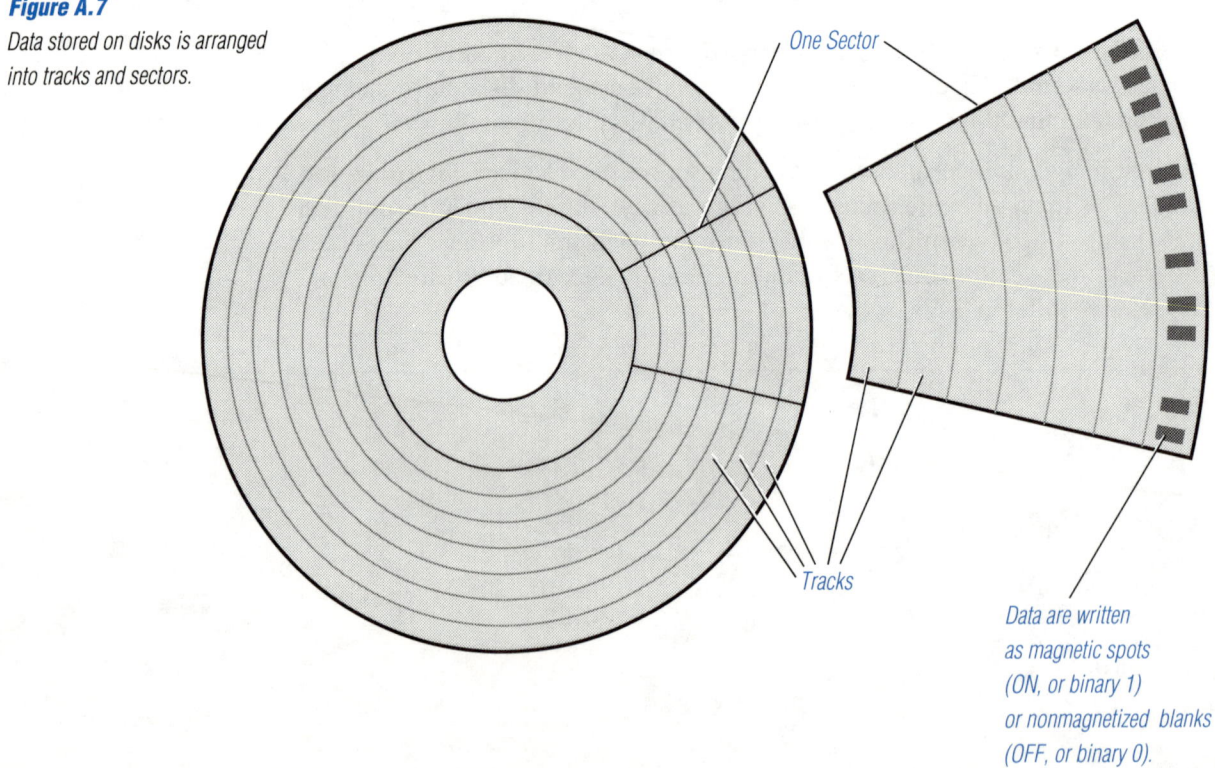

One Sector

Tracks

Data are written as magnetic spots (ON, or binary 1) or nonmagnetized blanks (OFF, or binary 0).

When you save a data or program file on disk, DOS adds the filename, extension, date, time, and other information to the disk directory. A total of 32 bytes (characters) are reserved in the disk directory for every entry. Listed below is a breakdown of the information stored in the disk directory for each file:

Character	Directory Entry
0-7	Filename
8-10	Extension
11	Attribute
	0 - Read Only
	1 - Hidden
	2 - System
	3 - Volume Label
	4 - Subdirectory
	5 - Archive
12-21	Reserved
22-23	Time
24-25	Date
26-27	Pointer (link to FAT)
28-31	File size in bytes

THE CARE AND PROTECTION OF YOUR DISKS

How can you measure the value of data stored on disk? Reports and proposals stored on disk media represent hundreds of hours of work that can never be exactly duplicated. A little common sense and care, as illustrated in Figure A.8, will go a long way in protecting this valuable data.

Figure A.8
Practical tips for protecting data stored on disks.

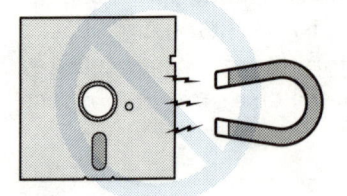

Never place diskettes near magnetic devices.

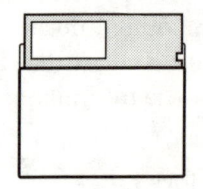

Always place diskettes back into a disk envelope when you are not using them.

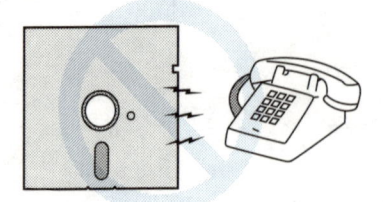

Keep diskettes away from the telephone.

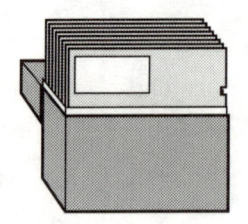

Store your diskettes in a safe place.

Never touch the floppy disk media.

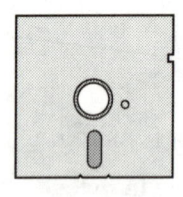

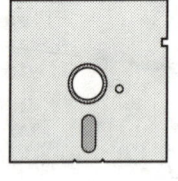

Always make backup copies of your data.

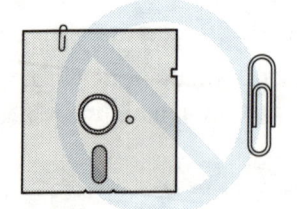

Don't use paper clips on disks.

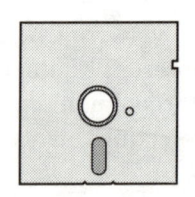

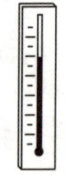

Store and use at temperatures between 50° and 110° F.

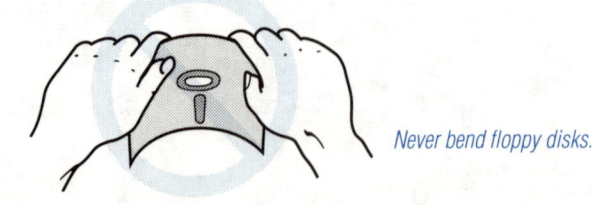

Never bend floppy disks.

Appendix B

DOS COMMANDS AND UTILITIES

I = Internal Command
E = External Utility

		CMD	UTY	2.x	3.0	3.1	3.2	3.3	4.0
APPEND	Data file search path		E				•	•	•
ASSIGN	Drive to drive assignment		E	P	•	•	•	•	•
ATTRIB	Define/Display file attributes		E		•	•	•	•	•
BACKUP	Backup hard disk		E	•	•	•	•	•	•
BREAK	Define Control-Break check	I		•	•	•	•	•	•
CHCP	Define page for COMMAND.COM	I						•	•
CHDIR (CD)	Change directory	I		•	•	•	•	•	•
CHKDSK	Check disk status		E	•	•	•	•	•	•
CLS	Clear screen	I		•	•	•	•	•	•
COMP	Compare file(s)		E	P	P	P	P	•	•
COPY	Copy file(s)	I		•	•	•	•	•	•
CTTY	Change command device		E	•	•	•	•	•	•
DATE	Set/Display system date	I		•	•	•	•	•	•
DEL	Delete file(s)	I		•	•	•	•	•	•
DIR	Display disk directory	I		•	•	•	•	•	•
DISKCOMP	Compare two disks		E	•	•	•	•	•	•
DISKCOPY	Copy disk		E	•	•	•	•	•	•
ERASE	Delete file(s)	I		•	•	•	•	•	•
EXE2BIN	Convert .EXE file to .COM file		E	•	•	•	•	•	•

P = PC DOS only   **M** = MS DOS only   • = Both

		CMD	UTY	2.x	3.0	3.1	3.2	3.3	4.0
EXIT	Terminate child shell	I		•	•	•	•	•	•
FASTOPEN	Speeds access to specific files							•	•
FC	Compare file(s)		E	M	M	M	M	M	M
FDISK	Configure hard disk		E	P	P	P	•	•	•
FIND	Locate characters within a file		E	•	•	•	•	•	•
FORMAT	Initialize a disk for use		E	•	•	•	•	•	•
GRAFTABL	Access to extended ASCII characters		E		•	•	•	•	•
GRAPHICS	Print graphics screen		E	M	M	M	•	•	•
JOIN	Join a drive to directory path		E		•	•	•	•	•
KEYBnn	Keyboard layout (nn=country)		E		P	P	•		
KEYB	Keyboard layout (keyboard.sys)		E					•	•
LABEL	Create/change disk label		E		P	•	•	•	•
MEM	Display free & allocated memory		E						P
MKDIR (MD)	Create directory	I		•	•	•	•	•	•
MODE	Configure device		E	P	P	P	•	•	•
MORE	Paginate filter for screen		E	•	•	•	•	•	•
NLSFUNC	National language support							•	•
PATH	Command search path	I		•	•	•	•	•	•
PRINT	Background file(s) printing		E	•	•	•	•	•	•
PROMPT	Define/change system prompt	I		•	•	•	•	•	•
RECOVER	Recover damaged file(s)		E	•	•	•	•	•	•
REN	Rename file(s)	I		•	•	•	•	•	•
REPLACE	Selectively replace/add file(s)		E				•	•	•
RESTORE	Restore hard disk from backup		E	•	•	•	•	•	•
RMDIR (RD)	Remove directory	I		•	•	•	•	•	•
SELECT	International keyboard command		E		P	P	P	•	•

P = PC DOS only **M** = MS DOS only • = Both

APPENDIX B **199**

		CMD	**UTY**	**2.x**	**3.0**	**3.1**	**3.2**	**3.3**	**4.0**
SET	Define environment variables	I		•	•	•	•	•	•
SHARE	File sharing		E				•	•	•
SORT	Alphabetically sort file data		E	•	•	•	•	•	•
SUBST	Substitute a drive for another		E				•	•	•
SYS	Transfer operating system		E	•	•	•	•	•	•
TIME	Set/Display system time	I		•	•	•	•	•	•
TREE	Display directory structure		E		P	P	•	•	•
TYPE	Display ASCII file to screen	I		•	•	•	•	•	•
VER	Display DOS version	I		•	•	•	•	•	•
VERIFY	Verify file copies	I		•	•	•	•	•	•
VOL	Display disk volume label	I		•	•	•	•	•	•
XCOPY	Copy directory tree and file(s)	I					•	•	•

Configuration Commands

		2.x	**3.0**	**3.1**	**3.2**	**3.3**	**4.0**
BREAK	Define Control-Break check	•	•	•	•	•	•
BUFFERS	Define number of disk buffers	•	•	•	•	•	•
COUNTRY	Define country-specific values	M	•	•	•	•	•
DEVICE	Load a device driver	•	•	•	•	•	•
DRIVPARM	Define drive parameters				M	M	M
FCBS	Define number of file control blocks		M	•	•	•	•
FILES	Define number of open files	•	•	•	•	•	•
INSTALL	Check for commands within CONFIG.SYS						P
LASTDRIVE	Define name of last drive		•	•	•	•	•
SHELL	Define command interpreter	•	•	•	•	•	•
STACKS	Define stack size				•	•	•
SWITCHES	Specifies use of conventional keyboard						P

P = *PC DOS only*   **M** = *MS DOS only*   • = *Both*

Configuration Files

		2.x	3.0	3.1	3.2	3.3	4.0
ANSI.SYS	Supports ANSI escape sequences	•	•	•	•	•	•
DISPLAY.SYS	Supports page switching for console					•	•
DRIVER.SYS	Supports external disk drives				•	•	•
KEYBOARD.SYS	Contains keyboard layouts					•	•
XMAEM.SYS	Emulates expanded memory						P
XMA2EM.SYS	Supports expanded memory specification						P
PRINTER.SYS	Supports page switching for ports					•	•
RAMDRIVE.SYS	Simulates disk drive in memory				M	M	M
VDISK.SYS	Same as RAMDISK.SYS		P	P	P	P	P

Batch Commands

		2.x	3.0	3.1	3.2	3.3	4.0
CALL	Call a batch file from a batch file					•	•
ECHO	Set display status	•	•	•	•	•	•
FOR	Perform a command for a set of files	•	•	•	•	•	•
GOTO	Transfer control	•	•	•	•	•	•
IF	Conditional check	•	•	•	•	•	•
PAUSE	Hold for user response	•	•	•	•	•	•
REM	Remark	•	•	•	•	•	•
SHIFT	Loop through replaceable parameters	•	•	•	•	•	•

P = PC DOS only   **M** = MS DOS only   **•** = Both

Appendix C

DOS RULES FOR NAMING FILES

Filenames must follow a few simple guidelines. DOS filenames must not exceed eight (8) characters in length, and the extension must not exceed three (3) characters. A filename of at least one (1) acceptable character is required to avoid a `File Creation Error`. Extensions, however, are optional. The general format is illustrated below:

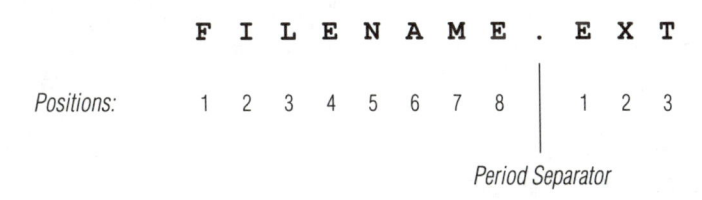

```
              F I L E N A M E . E X T
Positions:    1 2 3 4 5 6 7 8   1 2 3
                              |
                       Period Separator
```

NOTE: *Many software packages will add predefined extensions (default extensions) to user-indicated filenames. You may experience problems with these software packages if you force or rename an extension where a predefined extension is expected.*

It makes no difference to DOS if the filename is typed in upper case or lower case, since DOS will always convert the filename to upper case prior to acting on the filename.

DOS has some built-in safeguards that you should be aware of but should NEVER come to depend on. When a filename or extension exceeds its respective 8– or 3–character limit, DOS will truncate (drop off the end) the extra letters of the filename or extension so it falls within the proper limits.

User Typed	DOS Accepted
filename.ext	FILENAME.EXT
aaaaaaaaaaaa.123	AAAAAAAA.123
bbbbbbbbbbbb.bbbbb	BBBBBBBB.BBB
12345678901234	12345678
cC.cCcCcCcCcC	CC.CCC

ACCEPTABLE CHARACTERS FOR FILENAMES

Uppercase letters	A - Z
Lowercase letters	a - z
Numbers	0 - 9
Special symbols	$ % ^ ` - @ _ ( ) { } ` ' ! # ~

(The symbols / \ [ ] : ; | < > + = . , cannot be used.)

NOTE: *It is possible that some applications will not permit all the special characters listed above. Should you have any question about what is acceptable, use only letters and numbers.*

INVALID FILENAMES

Because DOS reserves some names for its own use in relating to specific devices, these names must be avoided as filenames. These reserved names are: AUX, CLOCK$, COM, CON, KYBD$, LPT, LST, NUL, PRN, SCRN$, and any command or utility names.

FILENAMING SYSTEMS

It is important that you develop a descriptive system for naming files. A well thought out filenaming system improves your ability to locate files at future dates. When consistently used, the system will enhance your ability to incorporate the wild card features into file searches.

Appendix D

PARALLEL AND SERIAL PORTS

Two basic types of input/output ports are used by microcomputers. Each has advantages and disadvantages regarding transmission speeds and reliable transmission distances, and you should be aware of their differences. They are the ***parallel*** and ***serial*** ports, and your computer configuration may have one or both. Ports will vary between female or male connectors and the number of connecting points, called ***pins.*** The female connector receives the male connector, and the two can usually be fastened together for a secure connection. In case of a hardware incompatiblity, ***gender changers*** are available to convert from male to female or vice versa.

Parallel Ports

Parallel ports provide the fastest transmission speeds, but attached hardware should be within 10 feet of the computer for reliable data transmission. The 25-pin arrangement illustrated in Figure D.1 represents a typical parallel port connector.

DOS references parallel ports as LPT, and sequentially numbers each port. Usually, a printer is attached to the first parallel port (LPT1).

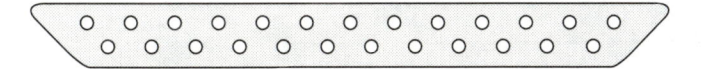

Figure D.1
The 25-pin connector generally used for the parallel port.

NOTE: *Serial ports may also use the pin configuration shown in Figure D.1. When the ports are not labeled, consult your owner's manual or the dealer who sold you the system. If your microcomputer has one 25-pin connector in the back, it is usually a parallel port.*

Serial Ports

Data transmission speeds through a ***serial port*** are slower than those associated with parallel ports. However, serial transmission provides reliable service for equipment up to 50 feet from the computer. You will find serial ports using both 25-pin or 9-pin connectors. Ports that handle serial data transmission are referenced by DOS as COM1, COM2, and so on.

Figure D.2
The 9-pin connector generally used for the serial port.

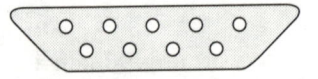

NOTE: *Special adapters are available for converting equipment between 25-pin and 9-pin port connectors.*

Differences in Data Transmisson

Parallel ports send information bits in parallel, a byte (8 bits) at a time. In serial transmission, the binary components of each data character are sent down a single transmission line, one after another. Figure D.3 graphically shows the difference between data transmission through serial and parallel ports.

Figure D.3
Parallel and serial ports use different methods to transmit data.

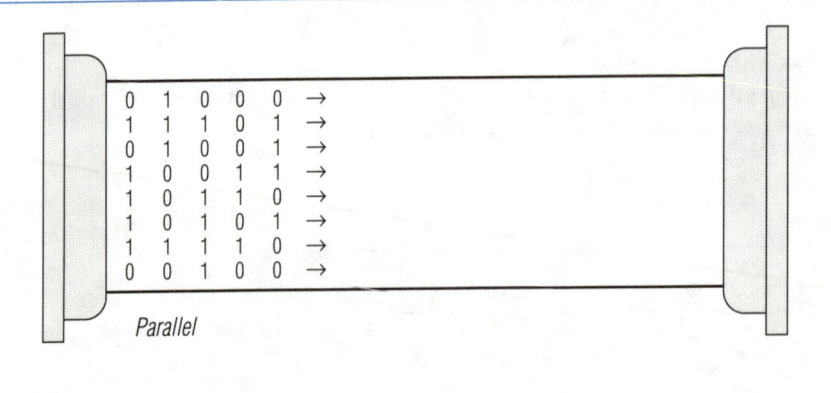

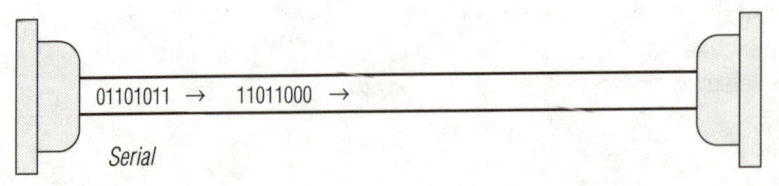

```
0 1 0 0 0 →
1 1 1 0 1 →
0 1 0 0 1 →
1 0 0 1 1 →
1 0 1 1 0 →
1 0 1 0 1 →
1 1 1 1 0 →
0 0 1 0 0 →
```
Parallel

01101011 →   11011000 →

Serial

Appendix E

PRACTICAL BATCH FILES

The batch files illustrated in this appendix are designed to access DOS external utility programs from a \DOS subdirectory found on drive C. The following batch file backs up the accounting software package described in Chapter 7.

ACCBAKUP.BAT

```
cd c:\account
c:\dos\backup c:\account a: /s /m
cd c:\
```

OTHER BATCH FILES OF INTEREST

These batch files use some advanced commands that are not covered in this DOS guide; nonetheless, they are presented for two reasons: first, beacause they are so useful; second, to pique your interest in learning to customize PC operations.

Root Directory Return

As long as your search path includes the BATCH subdirectory you can always get back to the root directory, even from a floppy drive, by simply entering R.

R.BAT

```
c:
cd c:\
cls
```

List and Pause

Type a file with the more utility filter active. You execute by typing LIST then a single blank space and the filename.ext you wish to display.

LIST.BAT

```
cls
type %1 | c:\dos\more
```

Protect Files

PROT.BAT file will set the READ ONLY attribute to "on" for the file indicated or for the files referenced through a wild card file name. This protects the indicated files from modification. Execute by typing PROT then a single blank space and the filename.ext to be protected.

PROT.BAT

```
if "%1" == "" goto MESSAGE
c:\dos\attrib +r %1
goto END
:MESSAGE
echo No File(s) indicated.
:END
```

Unprotect Files

The following screen shows how to remove the file protection established by PROT. Execute in the same fashion as PROT.

UNPROT.BAT

```
if "%1" == "" goto MESSAGE
c:\dos\attrib -r %1
goto END
:MESSAGE
echo No File(s) indicated.
:END
```

Hard Disk Protection

FORMAT.BAT is a must for all hard disk users. Its function is to protect from an accidental formatting of your hard disk.

NOTE: *This file makes some assumptions. The DOS format utility is in a subdirectory called \DOS. The DOS format utility has been renamed XFORMATX.EXE (or .COM).*

FORMAT.BAT

```
echo off
cls
if "%1" == "" goto ERROR
if %1 == A: goto OK
if %1 == a: goto OK
if %1 == B: goto OK
if %1 == b: goto OK
:ERROR
echo INVALID OR ABSENT PARAMETER
echo Please RE-ENTER command with at least
echo a valid drive specification.
goto END
:OK
c:\dos\xformatx.exe %1 %2 %3 %4
:END
```

Delete these two lines if your computer doesn't have drive B.

NOTE: *BACKUP with the /F switch will not use a batch file named FORMAT.BAT. As a result, this batch file disables the BACKUP /F switch offered with DOS versions 3.3 and newer.*

Appendix F

LOCAL AREA NETWORKS

The need to share information grows as the number of people using personal computers within an office or school increases. For an information-based work environment to be efficient and effective, microcomputer users need to share data-processing capabilities and common software. This is where a ***Local Area Network (LAN)*** comes into play. The LAN is the hardware that connects personal computer systems in a small geographic area, as in an office building or college campus. These interconnections, or ***connectivity***, enable users to quickly and easily share information, software, and output devices.

WHAT IS A LAN?

Simply put, a LAN, or Local Area Network, is a hardware system that connects two or more personal computers together with a common cable. The basic components of a LAN system include:

- Personal computers
- Network interface boards (one per computer)
- Cable
- Network software
- Designated person to be the Network Manager.

HOW DOES A LAN WORK?

Once the hardware is in place—the PCs, the interface boards, and associated cables—the key to making a LAN work is the software (under the supervision of the Network Manager). You will recall from Chapter 7 that the hardware/software realtionship is defined at three basic levels:

- BIOS (Basic Input Output System)
- DOS (Disk Operating System)
- Command interpreter (COMMAND.COM)

The LAN software fits into the system at the BIOS level. The network software has its own BIOS called NETBIOS which is added to the existing BIOS. The NETBIOS describes how the network hardware handles the input and output. Software is added at the DOS level as well.

DOS INSTRUCTIONS THAT DON'T WORK ON LANS

A personal computer (PC) connected to a LAN shares hardware resources with other computers. Therefore, personal computers can access files stored on other systems and output data to several printers linked to the LAN. This expanded hardware capacity does limit the scope or function of some of the DOS instructions described in this Guide. As a result, the following DOS instructions may not work with shared hardware connected to a LAN or will work in restricted ways:

CHKDSK

DISKCOMP

DISKCOPY

FORMAT

LABEL

RECOVER

SUBST

SYS

Glossary

Alt (alternate) key Key used in combination with other keys.

APPEND Identifies alternative search paths for data files.

application program Instructions a computer uses to perform a specific user-oriented task—for example, games, graphic arts, or printing paychecks.

ASCII American Standard Code for Information Interchange that identifies the internal format for basic text stored by computers.

ATTRIB Sets file attributes.

Backspace key Moves cursor to the left.

BACKUP Copies files of any size to the appropriate number of floppy disks or diskettes.

bad sectors Damaged areas on a disk's recording surface.

batch command Special DOS instructions used in a batch file.

batch file Collection of DOS instructions and batch commands in a file with a .BAT extension that are designed to be executed in sequence.

batch processing Executing a group of DOS instructions in sequence without unnecessary user intervention.

BIOS Basic Input Output System. A hidden file used to initially configure a microcomputer when it is booted.

booting Procedures for starting a microcomputer system.

Break= Configuration command used to instruct DOS to look for the Ctrl + Break key combination during all input or output activities.

buffer Temporary storage area in computer's main memory.

Buffers= Configuration command that changes the number of buffers used by DOS.

Caps Lock key Sets alphabetic keys into upper-case mode.

CD Changes the active disk directory.

CHDIR Changes the active disk directory.

CHKDSK Non-destructive examination of a disk that identifies bad segments, fragmented files, and lost data clusters.

CLS Clears screen.

COM Internal reference to a serial communication port.

command Instruction used by the disk operating system that is stored in the computer's memory for immediate execution.

command interpreter Designated system program that supervises memory, executes DOS commands, and loads DOS utility programs when needed. The program COMMAND.COM is the command interpreter for MS-DOS and PC-DOS.

CON DOS reserve word representing the keyboard for input and the screen for output.

configuration command Special DOS instructions used in a CONFIG.SYS file.

connectivity Ability to quickly and easily share data, programs, and peripheral equipment though the interconnection of computer systems.

COPY Transfers data or program files from one device to another.

Country= Configuration command that resets the international standards used with the keyboard, date and time.

Ctrl (control) key Key used in combination with other keys.

cursor Flashing line or box on a screen that shows where next character will appear.

data drive Drive containing the disk where data and application programs are stored (compare *system drive*).

DATE Changes the current date kept in the computer's memory.

default drive Disk drive DOS will use unless instructed otherwise.

DEL Erases a file from disk.

device driver System program that identifies operating characteristics of specific peripheral hardware.

Device= Configuration command that identifies which device drivers DOS should use.

DIR Displays disk directory on the screen.

disk directory Reserved track on a disk where information about files located on that disk are stored. This information includes the file's name, attributes, creation date, creation time, etc.

disk sector Disk storage area that is a subdivision of one disk track. Sectors are created when the disk is formatted.

disk track One of the concentric areas on a disk for storing data. Tracks are created when the disk is formatted.

DISKCOPY Duplicates the contents of one floppy disk onto another floppy disk.

DOS Disk operating system.

DOS commands Computer instructions used by the disk operating system that are stored in the computer's memory for immediate execution.

DOS prompt Screen display generated by the DOS command interpreter notifying the user that DOS is waiting for an instruction. In its default form, the DOS prompt is displayed as the letter associated with the default drive and the > symbol.

DOS utility program Computer instructions used by the disk operating system that are stored on disk.

Driveparm= Configuration command that changes default parameters associated with storage hardware.

Enter key Key that transmits instruction line or data to computer for processing when pressed. Also referred to as the Return key.

ERASE Deletes a file from disk.

Esc (escape) key Cancels current instruction.

expanded memory Memory beyond the usable DOS maximum of 640K used by application programs.

extended memory Specific memory addresses beyond the usable DOS maximum of 640K.

external utility program Computer instructions used by the disk operating system that are stored on disk.

F1 (function 1) key Recalls last instruction line one character at a time.

F3 (function 3) key Recalls remaining characters in last instruction line.

FCBS= Configuration command that sets the number of file control blocks used by DOS during disk input and output.

file allocation table (FAT) Index located on the disk track reserved for the disk directory that identifies where files are physically stored on that disk.

file attributes Special designations for a data or program file—for example, read-only, hidden, system, etc.

filename Means of identifying data and program instructions stored on disk or tape. DOS only accepts filenames of no more then eight characters and a three character extension—for example, TECBROC.TXT is an acceptable filename.

Files= Configuration command that sets the number of active files DOS can handle at one time.

FORMAT Initializes a new disk for use by computer system.

formatting Process of dividing a new disk into tracks and sectors and establishing the disk directory and file allocation table (FAT).

fragmented file Data or program file broken into several parts and stored on disk in physically separate locations.

function keys Series of keys, usually numbered from F1 to F10 or F12, that perform different operations depending on the software currently in control of the computer system.

gender changer Special connector that changes a female connector to male or vice versa.

global wild card character An asterisk (*) used to designate that any combination of characters within a filename is acceptable.

hardcopy Paper copy of output.

hidden file File that is not displayed as part of the disk directory.

icon Picture representing DOS operation.

initialization Process of dividing a new disk into tracks and sectors and establishing the disk directory and file allocation table (FAT). Also called formatting.

internal command Instruction used by the disk operating system that is stored in the computer's memory for immediate execution.

LABEL Changes the volume label on the designated disk.

LAN (local area network) A hardware system that connects personal computers in a small geographic area. Computers connected by a LAN can share data files, programs, and peripheral equipment.

Lastdrive= Configuration command that identifies how many active peripheral devices DOS will use.

lost cluster File segment not properly identified in the disk's file allocation table.

LPT Internal reference to a parallel port.

MD Makes a new subdirectory.

MEM Provides a memory status report.

MKDIR Makes a new subdirectory.

MODE Changes default setting associated with the screen, parallel ports, or serial ports.

MORE filter Special utility program used with TYPE command that allows only 24 lines at a time to be displayed on the screen.

MS-DOS Disk operating system developed by Microsoft (MS) for use with IBM and IBM-compatible microcomputers.

multi-tasking Ability to store and execute concurrently more than one program.

NUL DOS reserve word for "make believe" output device.

Num Lock key Key that activates the numeric functions on the numeric keypad. When deactivated, keys on the numeric keypad control cursor movement.

numeric keypad Separate sets of keys, usually at the extreme right side of the keyboard, which are laid out like a calculator keyboard with numbers, basic math functions, and Enter keys.

operating system Collection of system software that controls all the hardware within a specific computer system.

parallel port Connector used to attach peripheral equipment to a computer. In a parallel port, all eight bits of each byte (character) are transmitted at the same time (compare *serial port*).

PATH Identifies an alternate search path for finding program files that end with .EXE, .COM, or .BAT extensions.

PC-DOS IBM's personal computer (PC) disk operating system that is licensed from Microsoft and similar to Microsoft's MS-DOS.

peripheral Term describing equipment attached to the computer—for example, keyboards, screens, and disk drives.

physical drive Hardware being used as originally designed.

pins Connecting points on male ports or connectors.

presentation manager Graphics-oriented DOS shell.

PRINT Sends output to printer.

PRN DOS reserve word for printer attached to parallel port 1 (LPT1).

program Set of instructions the computer executes to perform a given task. Also called software.

PROMPT Changes the text used in the current DOS prompt.

queue Waiting list.

ram drive Utilizing memory to store files as if it were a disk drive.

RD Removes an empty subdirectory.

read-only file Data or program file that can be copied or used, but not erased or changed.

RECOVER Tries to recreate damaged files.

REN (RENAME) Changes a file's name in the designated disk directory.

REPLACE Selectively updates data or program files by copying a new version over an older one or by adding new files to a disk.

RESTORE Activates files stored with the BACKUP utility program.

Return key Transmits instruction line or data to computer for processing when pressed. Also referred to as the Enter key.

RMDIR Removes an empty subdirectory.

root directory Primary disk directory created when a disk is formatted.

scroll Method of displaying long files on a screen whereby new lines are added to the bottom while old lines are removed from the top.

Scroll Lock key Key used in combination with other keys.

search path Alternative disk directories where files could be located.

serial port Connector used to attach peripheral equipment to a computer. In a serial port, each bit of a byte (character) is sent sequentially, one after the other (compare *parallel port*).

shell Sophisticated menu that helps users construct DOS instruction lines.

Shell= Configuration command that reserves memory for the command interpreter or protects it from accidental erasure.

Shift key Key used in combination with other keys.

single character wildcard A question mark (?) within a filename that designates that any character is acceptable in that position.

soft-sectored disk Floppy disk or diskette with a single sensing hole which identifies the beginning of the disk tracks.

software Set of instructions the computer executes to perform given tasks. Also called computer program or program.

source drive Disk drive from which data or program instructions originate.

subdirectory File storage area subordinate to a disk's root directory.

Switches= Configuration command that forces DOS to treat an enhanced keyboard like a conventional IBM XT or IBM AT keyboard.

syntax Correct structure or arrangement of words in a DOS instruction.

system drive Drive containing the disk where DOS utility programs are stored (compare *data disk*).

system software Instructions a computer uses to oversee internal operations and peripheral activities.

target drive Disk drive receiving data or program instructions.

TIME Changes the current time kept in the computer's memory.

TYPE Sends file contents to screen.

updating Adding, changing, or deleting the contents of a data or program file.

utility program Computer instructions used by the disk operating system that are stored on disk.

VER Displays version number of system software currently in control of computer system.

VERIFY Checks that disk input and output activities have been completed without error.

virtual drive Hardware with a temporary assignment different from standard operating procedures—for example, memory can be a virtual drive when it is used to store files like a disk drive.

VOL Displays disk volume label, when it exists, from the designated disk.

warm boot Restarting a microcomputer by using the Ctrl + Alt + Del keys instead of physically turning the computer off and back on.

wild card character Symbol used for the location where any character is acceptable when identifying a filename.

write-protect notch Found on 5-1/4 inch floppy disks. When the write-protect notch is covered, data can be read from the disk, but not erased or changed.

write-protect window Found on 3-1/2 inch diskette. When the write-protect window is open, data can be read from the disk, but not erased or changed.

Index

DOS messages *are printed in color.*

Access denied
    REPLACE, 139
Alt (alternate) key, 37
    with Ctrl + Del, 29
APPEND, 103-105
    DOS Messages, 105
    cancel, 103, 105
    screens, 104-105
    syntax, 103
applications program, 1
Are you sure (Y/N)?, 61
    ERASE (DEL), 53
ASCII, 64, 81, 83
asterisk, 49
Attempted write-protect violation
    FORMAT, 11
ATTRIB, 141-143
    DOS Messages, 142-143
    screens, 141-142
    syntax, 141
AUTOEXEC.BAT, 166
    screen, 168

Bad command or file name, 43-44
    APPEND, 105
    ATTRIB, 142
    CLS, 19
    COPY, 23, 26, 28
    DIR, 18
    DISKCOMP, 135
    LABEL, 57, 60
    MORE, 67
    VER, 8
    VERIFY, 25
    VOL, 13

Bad or missing filename
    CHKDSK, 132
Bad or missing xxxx.sys
    CONFIG.SYS, 166
bad sectors, 124, 143
Backspace key, 36
BACKUP, 106-112
    DOS Messages, 111-112
    screens, 108-111
    switches, 107
    syntax, 106
    wild card characters, 107
    4.0 changes, 186-187
batch file
    AUTOEXEC.BAT, 64
batch processing, 156
beep, 58
BIOS, 156
booting, 2
    DOS Messages, 6
    internal procedures, 157, 167
Break key, 37
Break=, 156-158
    syntax, 156
Buffers=, 158-159
    syntax, 158
    4.0 changes, 189
buffer, 158
bytes in bad sectors
    FORMAT, 12

Cannot execute FORMAT
    BACKUP, 112
Caps Lock key, 38

CD, 92-94
    DOS Messages, 94
    screens, 93-94
    syntax, 92
CHDIR, 92-94
    DOS Messages, 94
    screens, 93-94
    syntax, 92
CHKDSK, 123-130
    DOS Messages, 128-129
    screens, 124, 126-128
    switches, 125
    syntax, 123
clear screen, 19
CLS, 19
    DOS Messages, 19
    screen, 19
column separator, 65, 84
COM, 74, 77-80
command, 8
command interpreter, 166
Compare error on cylinder X, side X
    DISKCOMP, 135
CON, 68-70, 82
    input (keyboard), 70
    output (screen), 68-69
    screens, 69, 70
    syntax, 68, 70
condensed print, 77-78
CONFIG.SYS, 155, 164
    DOS Messages, 166
    Screens, 165
configuration commands, 156-164
connectivity, 209
COPY, 19-23, 82
    DOS Messages, 22-23, 71-72
    screens, 20-22, 69-70, 71
    switches, 21, 147
    syntax, 20, 26, 68, 70
    wild card characters, 50-51
copying files, 19
    wild card characters, 50-51

Contains nn non-contiguous blocks
    CHKDSK, 129
Country=, 162-163
    conversions, 163
    syntax, 162
    4.0 changes, 189
Ctrl (control) key, 37
    with Alt + Del, 39
    with Break, 70, 81
    with C key, 39, 70, 81-82
    with Num Lock, 38, 40, 64, 82
    with P key, 39
    with S key, 40, 82
    with PrtSc, 39, 40, 42, 72
    with Scroll Lock, 37, 39
    with Z key, 70, 71
cursor, 36

data drive, 3
DATE, 47-48
    DOS Messages, 48
    screen, 47
default drive, 6
Del (delete) key, 41
    with Alt + Ctrl, 39
DEL, 51-53
    DOS Messages, 53
    screens, 52-53
    switch, 187
    syntax, 52
    wild card characters, 53
    4.0 changes, 187
Device=, 160-161
    syntax, 160
    typical drivers, 160
device driver, 155
DIR, 14-18
    DOS Messages, 17-18
    screens, 15-17
    switches, 15
    syntax, 14
disk directory, 14
disk operating system, 1

INDEX

disk sector, 193

disk track, 193

Disk error reading (or writing) drive x
   VOL, 13

Disk unsuitable for system disk
   FORMAT, 11

DISKCOMP, 133-136
   DOS Messages, 135
   screens, 134-135
   syntax, 133

DISKCOPY, 130-133
   DOS Messages, 132-133
   screens, 131-132
   syntax, 130

diskette
   booting from, 4

DOS, 1

DOS commands, 8

DOS prompt, 6

DOS utility program, 8

Drive letter must be specified
   FORMAT, 11

Drive not ready
   FORMAT, 12

Driveparm=, 161-162
   switches, 161
   syntax, 161

Duplicate file name
   RENAME, 55

Enter key, 33, 36

ERASE, 51-53
   DOS Messages, 53
   screen, 53
   switch, 187
   syntax, 52
   wild card characters, 53
   4.0 changes, 187

Errors found, F parameter not specified. Corrections will not be written to disk
   CHKDSK, 128

Error on list device indicates that it may be off-line. Please check it
   PRINT, 76

Esc (escape) key, 36

expanded memory, 179

extended error, 183-185
   codes, 184-185

extended memory, 179

external utility program, 8

F1 (function 1) key, 41

F3 (function 3) key, 41, 81

F6 (function 6) key, 70, 71

FAT. *See* file allocation table.

FCBS=, 163
   syntax, 163

file allocation table (FAT), 124, 144, 146, 193

File allocation table bad
   COPY, 23
   DIR, 17

File cannot be copied onto itself 27
   COPY, 22

File creation error
   COPY, 22
   RESTORE, 116

File not found, 28
   ATTRIB, 143
   COPY, 22, 71
   DEL, 53
   DIR, 18
   ERASE, 53
   RECOVER, 146
   RENAME, 55
   TYPE, 65

File not in PRINT queue
  PRINT, 76
Files=, 159-160
  syntax, 159
filename, 201
floppy disk
  booting from, 4
FORMAT, 8-12
  DOS Messages, 11-12
  screens, 10-11
  switches, 9, 187
  syntax, 9
  4.0 changes, 187-188
Format failure
  FORMAT, 11
formatting, 8
  3-1/2 inch diskette, 10
  5-1/4 inch floppy disk, 10
fragmented file, 124-125, 146
function keys, 33

gender changer, 203
global wild card character, 49
  screens, 50-51

hardcopy, 72
hidden file, 95, 156

icon, 190
Illegal device name
  MODE, 80
Incorrect DOS version
  SELECT, 178
indicator lights, 38
initialization, 8
  3-1/2 inch diskette, 10
  5-1/4 inch floppy disk, 10
initial booting procedures, 157, 167
Ins (insert) key, 41
Insufficient disk space
  COPY, 22, 72

Intermediate file error, 66
  MODE, 68
internal command, 8
Invalid argument
  BACKUP, 111
  RESTORE, 116
Invalid characters in volume label
  VOL, 12
  LABEL, 58
Invalid date
  DATE, 48
Invalid directory
  CD, 94
  MD, 90
  RD, 96
Invalid disk/diskette media
  SELECT, 178
Invalid drive or filename
  RECOVER, 146
Invalid drive specification
  CHKDSK, 133
  COPY, 23
  DIR, 18
  DISKCOMP, 135
  LABEL, 58
  VOL, 13
Invalid filename
  COPY, 71
  TYPE, 65
Invalid number of parameters, 29
  ATTRIB, 143
  CD, 94
  MD, 91
  RD, 94
Invalid parameter, 29
  BACKUP, 111
  CD, 94
  CHKDSK, 133
  COPY, 23
  DIR, 18
  DISKCOMP, 135
  MD, 91

PRINT, 76
RD, 96
RENAME, 55
RESTORE, 116
Invalid parameters on SELECT command line
SELECT, 178
Invalid path, not directory or directory not empty
RD, 96
Invalid search path
PATH, 102
Invalid SELECT boot media
SELECT, 178
Invalid time
TIME, 49

keyboard, 33-41
AT style, 34
enhanced 101-key, 35
error message, 42
portable, 35
XT style, 34

LABEL, 56-58
DOS Messages, 57-58
screens, 57
syntax, 56
LAN, 209
Last backup diskette not inserted
BACKUP, 112
Lastdrive=, 162
syntax, 162
left arrow, 36
local area network, 209
lost cluster, 125
LPT, 74, 77-80

MEM, 181-183
screens, 182-183
switch, 182
syntax, 181

MD, 88-91
DOS Messages, 90-91
screens, 89-90
syntax, 88
microcomputer
impact on productivity, 155
start-up procedures, 4
MKDIR, 88-91
DOS Messages, 90-91
screens, 89-90
syntax, 88
MODE, 77-80
DOS Messages, 80
screens, 78-80
syntax, 77, 78
MORE filter, 65-67, 83-84
DOS Messages, 67
screens, 66-67
syntax, 66
MS-DOS, 1
multi-tasking, 190
Must specify ON or OFF
VERIFY, 25

No appended directories
APPEND, 105
No files found 'A:\filename.ext'
No files added
REPLACE, 139
No files found 'A:\filename.ext'
No files replaced
REPLACE, 140
No retry on parallel printer time-out
PRINT, 76
No paper error writing device PRN
COPY, 71
Non-System disk or disk error, 6
Not able to backup (or restore) file
BACKUP, 112

INDEX

Not ready error reading (or writing) drive x
    COPY, 23
    DIR, 18
NUL, 147
Num Lock key, 38, 43
numeric keypad, 33

operating system, 1

parallel port, 203
Parameters not compatible
    FORMAT, 11
    REPLACE, 140
parse error, 183-185
    codes, 185
PATH, 100-103
    DOS Messages, 102
    cancel, 101-102
    screens, 101-102
    syntax, 100
Pause key, 40, 64
PC-DOS, 1
peripheral, 1
physical drive, 162
pins, 203
presentation manager, 190
PRINT, 72-76, 82-83
    DOS Messages, 76
    screens, 74-75
    switches, 73
    syntax, 73
PRINT queue is full
    PRINT, 76
Printer error
    MODE, 80
printer spacing, 77-79
PRN, 68
    screen, 70
program, 3
PROMPT, 97-100
    DOS Messages, 99-100
    screens, 98-99
    special characters, 97
    syntax, 97

question mark, 49
queue, 73

ram drive, 160
read-only file, 137, 140
RECOVER, 143-146
    DOS Messages, 146
    screens, 145
    syntax, 144
REN (RENAME), 54-55
    DOS Messages, 55
    screens, 55
    syntax, 54
REPLACE, 136-140
    DOS Messages, 139-140
    screens, 137-139
    switches, 136-137, 188
    syntax, 136
    4.0 changes, 188
Return key, 33, 36
    RD, 95-97
DOS Messages, 96
screens, 95-96
    syntax, 95
Reset Key, 39
RESTORE, 113-116
    DOS Messages, 116
    screens, 114-115
    switches, 113
    wild card characters, 114
Restore file sequence in error
    RESTORE, 116
RMDIR, 95-97
    DOS Messages, 96
    screens, 95-96
    syntax, 95
root directory, 85, 88, 91

scroll, 63
Scroll Lock key, 37, 38

INDEX

search path, 92, 100
SELECT, 178
   DOS Messages, 178
   screens, 180
serial port, 203
shell, 179
Shell=, 163-164
   switches, 164
   syntax, 164
   4.0 changes 183-185
Shift key, 37, 38, 42
   with PrtSc, 39, 40, 42, 72
single character wild card, 49
   screen, 50
soft-sectored disk, 193
software, 1
source drive, 20
Strike a key when ready..., 15
subdirectory, 85
switch, command use
   BACKUP (/S, /M, /A, /D, /F), 107
   CHKDSK (/F, /V), 125
   COPY (/V,), 21, (/B), 147
   DEL (/P), 187
   DIR (/P, /W), 15
   ERASE (/P), 187
   FORMAT (/V, /S, /B), 9, (/F), 187
   MEM (/PROGRAM), 182
   PRINT (/P, /C, /T, /Q), 73
   REPLACE (/A, /D), 136, (/P, /R, /S, /W), 137, (/U), 136, 188
   RESTORE (/S, /P), 113
   SHELL (/E, /P), 64, (/MSG, /P), 183
switch
   how to use, 9, 30
Switches=, 185 syntax, 26
Syntax error
   ATTRIB, 143
system date, 47, 60
system drive, 3
system software, 1
system time, 48

Target disk cannot be used for backup
   BACKUP, 112
Target disk is write protected
   CHKDSK, 132
   COPY, 22
Target disk may be unusable
   CHKDSK, 132
target drive, 20
telecommunications, 78
TIME, 48-49
   DOS Messages, 49
   screen, 48
   4.0 changes, 188-189
Track 0 bad - disk unusable
   FORMAT, 12
TYPE, 63-65, 72, 81-82
   DOS Messages, 65
   screens, 64
   syntax, 63

Unable to create directory
   MD, 90
Unable to use
   BACKUP, 112
Unrecognized command in CONFIG.SYS
   CONFIG.SYS, 166
updating, 47
utility program, 8

VER, 7-8
   DOS Messages, 8
   screens, 7
VERIFY, 24-25
   DOS Messages, 25
   screens, 24
   syntax, 24
virtual drive, 160, 162
VOL, 12-13
   DOS Messages, 13
   screens, 13
volume label, 12, 56

warm boot, 39

Warning! Diskette is out of sequence
   RESTORE, 113

wild card character,
   screens 50-51

Write protect error writing drive X, 28, 66
   COPY, 72
   LABEL, 58
   MORE, 67

write-protect notch, 191

write-protect window, 192